MARTA SKADSHEIM TORKILDSEN

Knitted Baby Blankets and Cuddle Bags

OVER 50 DESIGNS TO MAKE AND SHARE

TRAFALGAR SQUARE
North Pomfret, Vermont

First published in the United States of America
in 2020 by
Trafalgar Square Books
North Pomfret, Vermont 05053

Originally published in Norwegian as *Babytepper*.

The instructions and material lists in this book were carefully
reviewed by the author and editor; however, accuracy cannot be
guaranteed. The author and publisher cannot be held liable for
errors.

ISBN: 978-1-64601-035-6
Library of Congress Control Number: 2020943884

Interior Design/Layout: Johanne Hjorthol
Cover Design: RM Didier
Photography: Studio Hjelm, Stavanger
Translation into English: Carol Huebscher Rhoades

Printed in China
10 9 8 7 6 5 4 3 2 1

Table of Contents

Preface

My mother taught me how to knit when I was four years old—and I'll be forever grateful for her patience! Over the years, I've made countless blankets and garments of all sizes and shapes. The pleasures of knitting never get old; and one of the best of them, as my aunt rightly told me once, is to have something real you can hold in your hands when you're finished. Some patterns are so simple they practically knit themselves, and you can relax and let your thoughts wander. Others require your full concentration for every stitch you knit. Knitting can be demanding—but also unbelievably satisfying, when you get to enjoy the loveliness of the result.

Baby blankets are so much fun to knit, whether to keep or to give away. There's something extra special about being able to wrap a child up in handmade comfort, worked with love and care. Hand-knit blankets and cuddle bags will often last longer than anything you can buy in a store—long enough for multiple children to enjoy—and with all kinds of beautiful fibers and colors to work with, you can make something truly unique and personal.

This book is meant to be a source of inspiration, written with the hope that it will put some of the infinite possibilities of knitting at your fingertips. The patterns collected here vary in difficulty, from the delightfully simple to the more demanding. Some of the most elegant designs can be worked using only knitting and purling. Choose the pattern you like best, pick out your favorite colors, and enjoy yourself; be proud of the wonderful things you make!

Good luck.

Marta Skadsheim Torkildsen
Stavanger, September 2019

YARNS AND FIBERS

The patterns in this book use Merino wool, alpaca, or mulberry silk yarns. These yarns don't cause any itching for most people and will feel nice and soft against the skin.

Merino Wool
Merino wool comes from Merino sheep, a breed specially selected for its fine wool. Most people won't feel any skin irritation from Merino wool, as it's very soft. This makes it especially good for baby blankets.

Alpaca
Alpacas are hooved animals from the South American branch of the camelid family. Alpaca fiber is several times stronger and warmer than sheep's wool. It's not scratchy for most people and is especially soft against the skin. Alpaca fiber warms well when it's cold, and cools when it's hot.

Mulberry Silk
Mulberry silk is a cultivated fiber from silkworms raised in carefully controlled conditions. The name comes from the mulberry leaves these larvae eat. Once the larvae have fed on mulberry leaves for a month, they are full-grown, and will spin cocoons of raw silk around themselves. Each cocoon is composed of one continuous strand about 328-984 yd/300-900 meters long. Mulberry silk is often combined with alpaca to make a lustrous yarn.

Superwash
Superwash-treated wool can be machine-washed on a delicate or wool program.

YARN SUBSTITUTES

You can use a different yarn than that recommended in any pattern, but make sure you choose a yarn of the same thickness. A substitute yarn should have about the same yardage/meterage as the recommended yarn, in a skein or ball of the same weight.

Fine Merino wool yarn—CYCA #1 (fingering)
Viking Garn (Viking of Norway) Baby Ull, 100% superwash Merino wool, 50 g = approx. 191 yd/175 m
Garnstudio Drops Baby Merino, 100% superwash Merino wool, 50 g = approx. 191 yd/175 m
Gjestal Merino Babyull, 100% superwash Merino wool, 50 g = approx. 191 yd/175 m
Dale Garn Baby Ull, 100% superwash Merino wool, 50 g = approx. 180 yd/165 m
Sandnes Garn Babyull Lanett, 100% superwash Merino wool, 50 g = approx. 191 yd/175 m
Trysil Babygarn, 100% superwash Merino wool, 50 g = approx. 191 yd/175 m

Medium-weight Merino wool yarn—CYCA #3 (DK, light worsted)
Garnstudio Drops Merino Extra Fine, 100% superwash Merino wool, 50 g = approx. 115 yd/105 m
Gjestal Pure Merino, 100% superwash Merino wool, 50 g = approx. 115 yd /105 m
Sandnes Garn Merinoull, 100% superwash Merino wool, 50 g = approx. 114 yd/104 m
Trysil 100% Merino, 100% superwash Merino wool, 50 g = approx. 115 yd /105 m

Alpaca—CYCA #1 (fingering) or CYCA #2 (sport baby)
Sandnes Garn Mini Alpakka, 100% alpaca, 50 g = approx. 164 yd/150 m (fingering)
Garnstudio Drops Alpaca 100% alpaca, 50 g = 183 yd/167 m (sport)
Du Store Alpakka, Tynn Alpakka, 100% alpaca, 50 g = approx. 183 yd /167 m (fingering)

Alpaca and Silk
Sandnes Garn Alpakka-Silke, 70% alpaca, 30% mulberry silk, 50 g = approx. 219 yd /200 m (fingering)
Garnstudio Drops Baby Alpaca Silk, 70% baby alpaca, 30% mulberry silk, 50 g = approx. 183 yd /167 m (sport)

KNITTING TIPS

- **Begin the piece** by casting on over two needles of the same size, held together. This ensures the edge won't be too tight. After casting on, carefully remove one needle.

- **Change to a new ball** at the outer edge of the piece to avoid a join in the middle of a row. It's easier to weave in ends from the edge, and makes a smoother join.

- **A knot in the yarn:** You might sometimes find a knot or splice in your yarn. In that case, cut the yarn at the end of a row, removing the length that includes the knot or splice, and start a new strand at the beginning of the next row.

- **Changing colors within a row:** Twist the strands around each other at each color change to avoid holes.

- **Weaving in yarn in a crocheted edging:** If you're going to crochet an edging around a blanket, don't weave in the ends until you've finished crocheting the edging. It will look best that way—and it'll be easier, too.

- **Round yarns** plied with several strands produce the clearest pattern structure for knit and purl relief stitch patterns. Each stitch will pop out nicely. For this type of patterning, it's better to work a little tightly than too loosely.

ABBREVIATIONS

BO	bind off (= British cast off)	m	meters	sl m	slip marker
ch	chain st	mm	millimeters	ssk	(sl 1 knitwise) 2 times, insert
cm	centimeter(s)	p	purl		left needle left to right
CO	cast on	pm	place marker		through the 2 sts and knit
dc	double crochet (= British treble crochet)	psso	pass slipped st over		together through back loops = left-leaning decrease
		rem	remain(s) (ing)		
g	grams	rep	repeat	st(s)	stitch(es)
in	inch(es)	rnd(s)	round(s)	tbl	through back loop(s)
k	knit	RS	right side	WS	wrong side
k2tog	knit 2 together = right-leaning decrease	sc	single crochet (= British double crochet)	yd	yards
		sl	slip	yo	yarnover

CHARTS

Charts show the right side of a knitting project. The chart is read from right to left for right-side rows, or left to right for wrong-side rows. Begin at the lower right corner. Each square represents a stitch. The symbol in the square shows how the stitch should be worked. Follow the symbols key next to the chart. As a general rule, charts show one repeat of the pattern, or a pattern sequence which can be repeated several times. In order to keep track of where you are in the pattern, you can use a ruler and magnetic board to mark your place. Move the ruler up each row, line by line; each line on the chart shows one row of knitting. Be careful to accurately track the rows you've done.

X	X	X	X	X	X	X	X	X	X	X	X	X	X	X	X	X
X	X	X	X	X	X	X	X	X	X	X	X	X	X	X	X	X
/	/	/	O		O		O		O		O		O	/	/	/

	= knit on RS, purl on WS
X	= purl on RS, knit on WS
O	= yo
/	= k2tog

SKILL LEVEL

Every pattern in this book includes a number of yarn balls; the number indicates the skill level needed to knit the design.

1 ball—easy

2 balls—intermediate

3 balls—experienced

INSPIRATION

Use your imagination and have fun. Choose the yarn fiber, color, and pattern to suit your own taste. The blanket colors in this book are only suggestions; if you like the way they look in the pattern photos, use the same colors! If you don't, don't. If you're knitting for someone else, consider discussing color choices with them, so you can be certain they'll love their gift. Using the book's patterns as a starting point, you can make any blanket large enough for a throw or bed blanket. Or make matching blankets in different colors at any size, for older sisters and brothers.

By using heavier yarn and larger needles, you can make a blanket just a little larger than the measurements given in the pattern. Size can also be adjusted by changing the number of stitches. Don't forget: if you're knitting a blanket with a pattern that repeats over a certain number of stitches, the total stitch count must be a multiple of that number of stitches, if you want the pattern repeats to work out evenly.

You can also knit longer rows, or use small blankets as squares to sew together for a larger blanket. You can even work two blankets and join them to create a matching pillow cover, if you like.

BLANKET CARE

Sometimes a knitted piece will draw in a bit as you knit it. When you're finished, you can lightly steam press the piece to stretch it back into shape. The stitches will look nice and even once you steam press them. But don't steam press the surface of a wool blanket directly. Lay the blanket on an ironing board, cover it with a damp pressing cloth, and, with iron set on low, press gently over the area covered by the cloth.

If the blanket's knitted with a relief stitch pattern, place it between two damp towels and leave it until completely dry. This is gentler than pressing, and the structure in the pattern will hold its shape instead of ending up pressed flat.

Superwash-treated wool can be machine-washed. Other types of yarns can also be machine-washed with care. Today's washing machines often have gentle programs for washing wool and silk.

- Machine-wash on wool/delicate program
- Maximum temperature of 86°F/ 30°C
- Use wool/silk-safe soap (for example, Eucalan or Soak)
- Do not use fabric softener
- Dry flat

Baby Blankets

There will always be a need for blankets for babies, and a hand-knit blanket is a fantastic gift to receive. It's also a relaxing project for anyone about to become a mother. It will be a lasting, loving memory to revisit for years to come.

You can never have enough baby blankets! Knit a blanket to go with a set of clothes for the newborn, a blanket for the baby carriage, and of course a blanket for the crib, too. It's so nice to have several blankets in a variety of materials, colors, and patterns.

#

FINISHED MEASUREMENTS

Approx. 32¼ x 37 in / 82 x 94 cm

MATERIALS

Yarn:

CYCA #2 (sport, baby)

Garnstudio Drops Alpaca (100% alpaca, 183 yd/167 m / 50 g)

Yarn Color and Amount:

Natural White 100: 350 g

Needles:

U. S. size 1.5 / 2.5 mm: 32 in / 80 cm circular

Crochet Hook:

U. S. size B-1/C-2 / 2.5 mm for edging

STITCHES AND TECHNIQUES

Garter Stitch

Knit back and forth on circular needle. Knit all rows. 2 rows = 1 ridge.

Pattern

Each block with heart motif is 21 sts across and 30 rows in length. 4 sts between each heart block are knitted in garter st ridges, and there are 8 rows (4 ridges) garter st between each tier of heart blocks.

Crocheted Edging

Work 1 sc, *ch 2, 1 dc in same ridge/st as sc, skip 1 ridge/st, 1 sc in next ridge/st*. Rep from * to * all around the blanket.

- The blanket is worked back and forth on a circular needle.
- CO 181 sts.
- Knit 6 ridges (= knit 12 rows).
- Always knit the outermost 5 sts on each row as edge sts.
- The pattern is worked over the center 171 sts between edge sts.
- Work charted pattern 9 times = 9 blocks in length.
- Finish with 6 garter ridges (= knit 12 rows).
- BO loosely.
- Crochet edging all around blanket.
- Weave in all ends neatly on WS.
- Block by gently steam pressing blanket on WS, under a damp pressing cloth.

	= knit on RS, purl on WS
x	= purl on RS, knit on WS
o	= yo
/	= k2tog
\	= sl 1, k1, psso (or ssk)
A	= sl 1, k2tog, psso (double decrease)

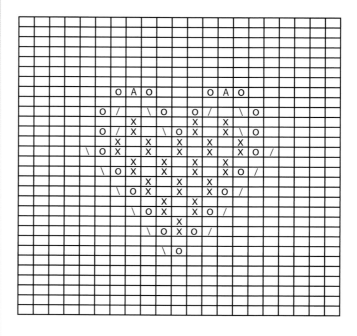

FINISHED MEASUREMENTS

Approx. 32¼ x 36¼ in /
82 x 92 cm

MATERIALS

Yarn:
CYCA #1 (fingering)
Garnstudio Drops Baby Merino
(100% superwash Merino wool,
191 yd/175 m / 50 g)

Yarn Color and Amount:
Purple Orchid 39: 400 g

Needles:
U. S. size 2.5 / 3 mm: 32 in / 80
cm circular

Crochet Hook:
U. S. size B-1/C-2 / 2.5 mm for
edging

STITCHES AND TECHNIQUES

Seed Stitch
Row 1: *K1, p1*; rep * to * across.
Row 2: Work knit over purl and purl over knit.
Rep Rows 1-2.

Crocheted Edging
NOTE: At the beginning of every rnd, ch 2 to substitute for 1 dc.
Rnd 1: *1 dc, ch 1*; rep * to * around. Insert hook in every other row or every other st all the way around. At each corner, rep * to * 2 times in the same st. End rnd with 1 sl st into top of turning ch.
Rnd 2: 1 sl st into ch, *1 dc in ch, ch 1*; rep * to * around. In each corner, work * to * 2 times in same st. End rnd with 1 sl st into top of turning ch.
Rnd 3: 1 sl st into ch, *(1 dc in ch, ch 1, 1 dc) in ch*; rep * to * around. End rnd with 1 sl st into top of turning ch.
Rnd 4: 1 sl st into ch, *1 dc, 1 picot (= ch 4, 1 sc in 1st ch), 1 dc in same ch as 1st dc*; rep * to * around. End rnd with 1 sl st into top of turning ch.

- The blanket is worked back and forth on a circular needle.
- CO 155 sts.
- Work in seed st until blanket is approx. 33½ in / 85 cm long.
- BO loosely.
- Crochet edging all around blanket.
- Weave in all ends neatly on WS.
- Block by gently steam pressing blanket on WS, under a damp pressing cloth.

Gro

FINISHED MEASUREMENTS
Approx. 31$^1/_2$ x 35$^1/_2$ in / 80 x 90 cm

MATERIALS
Yarn:
CYCA #1 (fingering) Viking Garn
Baby Ull (100% Merino wool, 191
yd/175 m / 50 g)
Yarn Color and Amount:
Natural White 302: 350 g
Needles:
U. S. size 6 / 4 mm: 32 in / 80 cm
circular
The blanket is intentionally worked
on a large needle, so it will be light
and airy.

STITCHES AND TECHNIQUES
Garter Stitch
Knit back and forth on circular
needle. Knit all rows. 2 rows = 1
ridge.

Pattern
See chart.

- The blanket is worked back and forth on a circular needle.
- CO 168 sts.
- Begin each row by slipping 1st st knitwise.
- Knit 6 ridges (= knit 12 rows).
- Always knit the outermost 6 sts on each row as edge sts.
- The pattern is worked over the center 156 sts between edge sts.
- Work in charted pattern until blanket is approx. 34 in / 86 cm long. End with a completed block.
- Finish with 6 ridges (= knit 12 rows).
- BO loosely.
- Weave in all ends neatly on WS.
- Block by gently steam pressing blanket on WS, under a damp pressing cloth.

☐ = knit on RS, purl on WS
X = purl on RS, knit on WS

		X	X
		X	X
X	X		
X	X		

Sanne

FINISHED MEASUREMENTS
Approx. 30 x 36¼ in / 76 x 92 cm

MATERIALS
Yarn:
CYCA #1 (fingering) Viking Garn Baby Ull (100% Merino wool, 191 yd/175 m / 50 g)
Yarn Color and Amount:
Pale Pink 364: 350 g
Needles:
U. S. size 6 / 4 mm: 32 in / 80 cm circular
The blanket is intentionally worked on a large needle, so it will be light and airy.

STITCHES AND TECHNIQUES
Garter Stitch
Knit back and forth on circular needle. Knit all rows. 2 rows = 1 ridge.

Stockinette Stitch
Knit on RS rows and purl on WS rows.

Pattern
K7 (garter st), *3 sts stockinette, k6 (garter st); rep * to * across, ending with 3 sts stockinette and 7 sts garter st.

- The blanket is worked back and forth on a circular needle.
- CO 170 sts.
- Begin each row by slipping 1st st knitwise.
- Knit 7 ridges (= knit 14 rows).
- Work in pattern until blanket is approx. 34¾ in / 88 cm long.
- Finish with 7 ridges (= knit 14 rows).
- BO loosely.
- Weave in all ends neatly on WS.
- Block by gently steam pressing blanket on WS, under a damp pressing cloth.

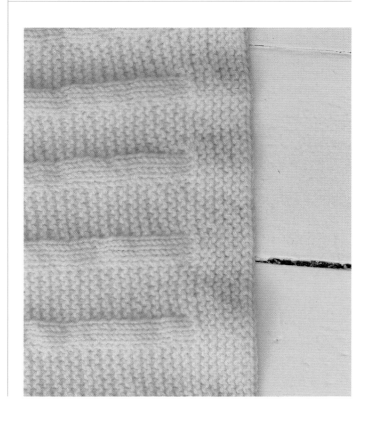

Solveig

FINISHED MEASUREMENTS
Approx. 31 x 36¾ in / 79 x 93 cm

MATERIALS
Yarn:
CYCA #1 (fingering) Viking Garn Baby Ull (100% Merino wool, 191 yd/175 m / 50 g)
Yarn Color and Amount:
Yellow 342: 350 g
Needles:
U. S. size 6 / 4 mm: 32 in / 80 cm circular
The blanket is intentionally worked on a large needle, so it will be light and airy.

STITCHES AND TECHNIQUES
Garter Stitch
Knit back and forth on circular needle. Knit all rows. 2 rows = 1 ridge.

Stockinette Stitch
Knit on RS rows and purl on WS rows.

Pattern
Rows 1-24: K7 (garter), *3 sts stockinette, k6 (garter)*; rep * to * across, ending with 3 sts stockinette, k7.
Rows 25-32: Knit every row = 4 garter ridges (= knit 8 rows).
Rep Rows 1-32.

- The blanket is worked back and forth on a circular needle.
- CO 170 sts.
- Begin each row by slipping 1st st knitwise.
- Knit 12 ridges (= knit 24 rows).
- Work in pattern until blanket is approx. 34¾ in / 88 cm long (ending with Row 24 in pattern).
- Finish with 12 ridges (= knit 24 rows).
- BO loosely.
- Weave in all ends neatly on WS.
- Block by gently steam pressing blanket on WS, under a damp pressing cloth.

Rafael

FINISHED MEASUREMENTS
Approx. 30¾ x 37½ in /
78 x 95 cm

MATERIALS
Yarn:
CYCA #1 (fingering) Sandnes
Garn Alpakka Silke (70% baby
alpaca, 30% mulberry silk, 219
yd/200 m / 50 g)
Yarn Colors and Amounts:
Blue-Green 7212: 200 g
White 1002: 100 g
Needles:
U. S. size 2.5 / 3 mm: 32 in / 80 cm
circular
Crochet Hook:
U. S. size B-1/C-2 / 2.5 mm for
edging

STITCHES AND TECHNIQUES
Garter Stitch
Knit back and forth on circular
needle. Knit all rows. 2 rows = 1
ridge.

Crocheted Edging
Rnd 1, Blue-Green: Work sc all
around the edge with 3 sc in each
corner st.
Rnd 2, White: 1 sc, *ch 3, skip
1 sc, 1 sc in next sc*; rep * to *
around.

- The blanket is worked back and forth on a circular needle.
- With Blue-Green, CO 174 sts.
- Knit 4 ridges (= knit 8 rows) with Blue-Green and then knit 2 ridges (= 4 rows) with White. Rep these stripes until blanket is approx. 36¾ in / 93 cm long.
- Knit 4 ridges (= knit 8 rows) with Blue-Green
- BO loosely.
- Crochet edging all around blanket.
- Weave in all ends neatly on WS.
- Block by gently steam pressing blanket on WS, under a damp pressing cloth.

Håkon

FINISHED MEASUREMENTS
Approx. 35 x 35 in / 89 x 89 cm

MATERIALS
Yarn:
CYCA #1 (fingering) Sandnes Garn Alpakka Silke (70% baby alpaca, 30% mulberry silk, 219 yd/200 m / 50 g)
Yarn Color and Amount:
Blue-Green 7212: 300 g
Needles:
U. S. size 2.5 / 3 mm: 32 in / 80 cm circular
Crochet Hook:
U. S. size B-1/C-2 / 2.5 mm for edging

STITCHES AND TECHNIQUES
Garter Stitch
Knit back and forth on circular needle. Knit all rows. 2 rows = 1 ridge.

Crocheted Edging
Work 1 sc in ridge, *ch 2, 2 dc in same ridge as sc, skip 1 ridge, 1 sc in next ridge*; rep * to * in every other ridge around.

- The blanket is knitted in garter st from corner to corner.
- CO 3 sts. Continue in garter st.
- At beginning of every row, increase 1 st with k1, yo, and then knit to end of row. On next row, work yarnover as k1tbl. Rep increase at beginning of every row.
- Continue as est until blanket measures 35 in / 89 cm on each side.
- Knit 1 ridge (= knit 2 rows) without increasing. Begin decreasing. At beginning of every row, k1, k2tog and then knit to end of row. Decrease as est until 5 sts rem.
- K1, sl 1, k2tog, psso, k1 = 3 sts rem.
- BO loosely.
- Crochet edging all around blanket.
- Weave in all ends neatly on WS.
- Block by gently steam pressing blanket on WS, under a damp pressing cloth.

Ida

FINISHED MEASUREMENTS
Approx. 33 x 34 in / 84 x 86 cm

MATERIALS
Yarn:
CYCA #1 (fingering) Viking Garn Baby Ull (100% Merino wool, 191 yd/175 m / 50 g)
Yarn Color and Amount:
Pale Pink 364: 300 g
Needles:
U. S. size 2.5 / 3 mm: 32 in / 80 cm circular

STITCHES AND TECHNIQUES
Garter Stitch
Knit back and forth on circular needle. Knit all rows. 2 rows = 1 ridge.

Pattern
The pattern consists of two different blocks. Each block has 25 stitches and 36 rows. Begin with block 1 and then work block 2. Alternate blocks 1 and 2 across. On the next tier, stagger the blocks.

1	2	1	2	1	2	1
2	1	2	1	2	1	2
1	2	1	2	1	2	1
2	1	2	1	2	1	2
1	2	1	2	1	2	1
2	1	2	1	2	1	2
1	2	1	2	1	2	1

- The blanket is worked back and forth on a circular needle.
- CO 195 sts.
- Begin each row by slipping 1st st knitwise.
- Knit 10 ridges (= knit 20 rows).
- The outermost 10 sts at each side are edge sts and always knitted on every row. The pattern is worked over the center 175 sts between edge sts.
- Work in pattern until blanket has 7 blocks in length.
- Finish with 10 ridges (= knit 20 rows).
- BO loosely.
- Weave in all ends neatly on WS.
- Block by patting blanket to finished measurements on a damp towel. Place another damp towel on top and leave until completely dry.

☐ = knit on RS, purl on WS
x = purl on RS, knit on WS

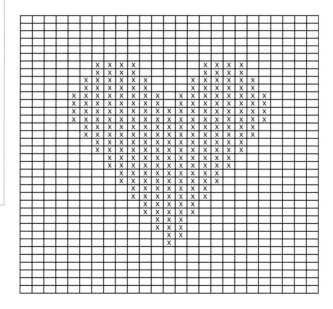

Block 1: Heart (see chart).

Block 2: Purl on RS and knit on WS (= reverse stockinette).

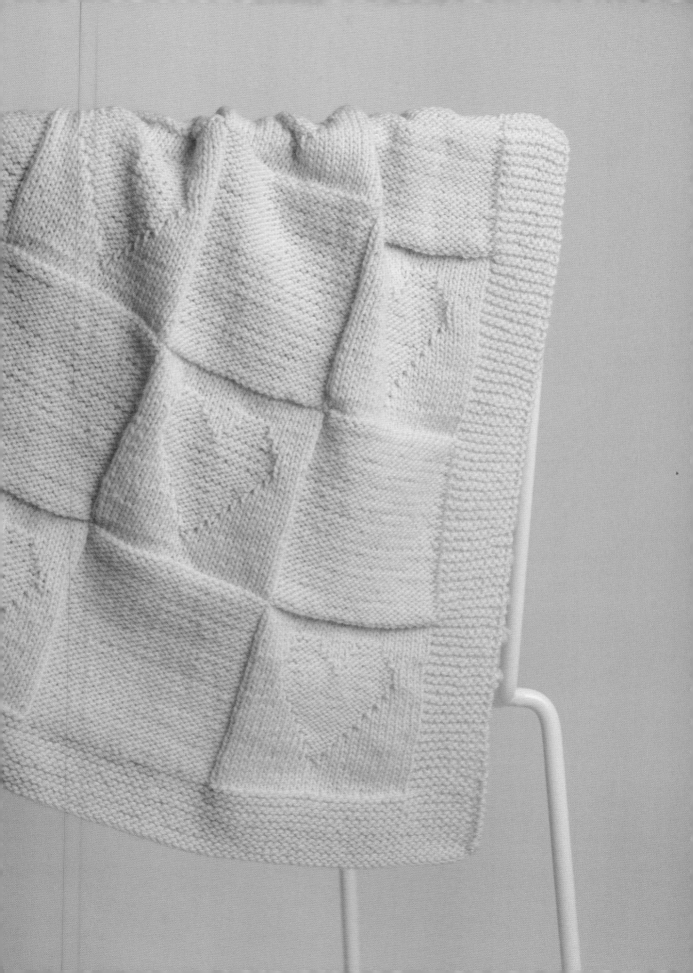

FINISHED MEASUREMENTS

Approx. 30¼ x 33½ in / 77 x 85 cm

MATERIALS

Yarn:
CYCA #1 (fingering) Viking Garn Baby Ull (100% Merino wool, 191 yd/175 m / 50 g)

Yarn Color and Amount:
Light Blue 320: 350 g

Needles:
U. S. size 2.5 / 3 mm: 32 in / 80 cm circular

STITCHES AND TECHNIQUES

Garter Stitch

Knit back and forth on circular needle. Knit all rows. 2 rows = 1 ridge.

Pattern

See chart. Each block with fish motif has 32 stitches and 24 rows. There are 5 garter sts between each fish block and 15 ridges (= knit 30 rows) between each tier of fish blocks.

- The blanket is worked back and forth on a circular needle.
- CO 173 sts.
- Knit 15 ridges (= knit 30 rows).
- The outermost 15 sts at each side are edge sts and always knitted on every row. The pattern is worked over the center 143 sts.
- Work in pattern until blanket has 6 blocks in length.
- Finish with 15 ridges (= knit 30 rows).
- BO loosely.
- Weave in all ends neatly on WS.
- Block by patting blanket to finished measurements and gently steam pressing blanket on WS, under a damp pressing cloth.

☐ = knit on RS, purl on WS
☒ = purl on RS, knit on WS

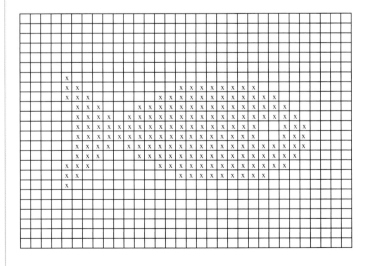

FINISHED MEASUREMENTS
Approx. 33 x 37¾ in / 84 x 96 cm

MATERIALS
Yarn:
CYCA #1 (fingering) Viking
Garn Baby Ull (100% Merino
wool, 191 yd/175 m / 50 g)
Yarn Color and Amount:
Yellow 342: 400 g
Needles:
U. S. size 2.5 / 3 mm: 32 in / 80 cm
circular
Crochet Hook:
U. S. size B-1/C-2 / 2.5 mm for
edging

STITCHES AND TECHNIQUES
Garter Stitch
Knit back and forth on circular
needle. Knit all rows. 2 rows = 1
ridge.

Pattern
See chart. Each block with star
motif has 39 stitches and 54 rows.
There are 5 garter sts between
each star block and 4 ridges
(= knit 8 rows) between each tier
of star blocks.

Crocheted Edging
1 sc, *ch 2, 1 dc in same ridge/
st as sc, skip 1 ridge/st, 1 sc in
next ridge/st*; rep from * to * all
around outer edge of blanket.

- The blanket is worked back and forth on a circular needle.
- CO 191 sts.
- Knit 10 ridges (= knit 20 rows).
- The outermost 10 sts at each side are edge sts and always knitted on every row. The pattern is worked over the center 171 sts.
- Work in pattern until blanket has 5 blocks in length.
- Finish with 10 ridges (= knit 20 rows).
- BO loosely.
- Crochet edging all around blanket.
- Weave in all ends neatly on WS.
- Block by patting blanket to finished measurements and gently steam pressing blanket on WS, under a damp pressing cloth.

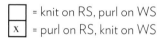

= knit on RS, purl on WS

x = purl on RS, knit on WS

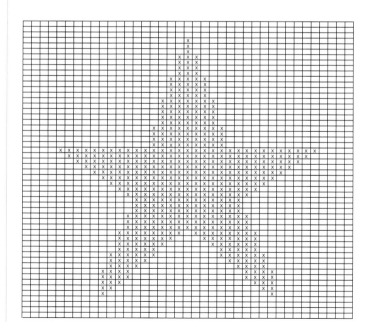

Torkel

FINISHED MEASUREMENTS
Approx. 31 x 34 in / 79 x 86 cm

MATERIALS
Yarn:
CYCA #1 (fingering) Gjestal Merino Babyull (100% superwash Merino wool, 191 yd/175 m / 50 g)
Yarn Color and Amount:
White 801: 400 g
Needles:
U. S. size 1.5 / 2.5 mm: 32 in / 80 cm circular
Crochet Hook:
U. S. size A/0 / 2 mm for edging

STITCHES AND TECHNIQUES
Seed Stitch
Row 1: *K1, p1*; rep * to * across.
Row 2: Work knit over purl and purl over knit.
Rep Rows 1-2.

Pattern
See chart.

Crocheted Edging
1 sc, *ch 2, 1 dc in same st as sc, skip ⅜ in / 1 cm, 1 sc in next st*; rep from * to * all around outer edge of blanket.

- The blanket is worked back and forth on a circular needle.
- CO 226 sts.
- Work in seed st for 2 in / 5 cm.
- The outermost 10 sts at each side are edge sts and always worked in seed st. The pattern is worked over the center 206 sts between edge sts.
- Work in pattern until blanket measures approx. 32 in / 81 cm in length. End with a complete pattern repeat.
- On next row, work 10 sts seed st, k206, work 10 sts in seed st.
- Finish with 2 in / 5 cm seed st.
- BO loosely.
- Crochet edging all around blanket.
- Weave in all ends neatly on WS.
- Block by patting blanket to finished measurements on a damp towel. Place another damp towel on top and leave until completely dry.

□ = knit on RS, purl on WS
X = purl on RS, knit on WS

X	X			X	X	X	X	X	X		X	X
X	X			X	X	X	X	X	X		X	X
X	X			X	X	X	X	X	X		X	X
X	X	X	X	X	X		X	X	X	X	X	X
X	X	X	X	X	X		X	X	X	X	X	X
X	X	X	X	X	X		X	X	X	X	X	X

repeat

Isabel

FINISHED MEASUREMENTS
Approx. 30 x 34 in / 76 x 86 cm

MATERIALS
Yarn:
CYCA #1 (fingering) Viking Garn Baby Ull (100% Merino wool, 191 yd/175 m / 50 g)
Yarn Colors and Amounts:
White 300: 250 g
Light Purple 377: 100 g
Needles:
U. S. size 6 / 4 mm: 32 in / 80 cm circular
The blanket is intentionally worked on a large needle, so it will be light and airy.
Crochet Hook:
U. S. size D-3 / 3 mm for edging

STITCHES AND TECHNIQUES
Garter Stitch
Knit back and forth on circular needle. Knit all rows. 2 rows = 1 ridge.

Pattern
See chart.

Crocheted Edging
Rnd 1: Work sc all around edge, with 3 sc in each corner st.
Rnd 2: 1 sc, *ch 2, 1 dc in same st as sc, skip 1 st, 1 sc in next st*; rep * to * around.

- The blanket is worked back and forth on a circular needle.
- With Light Purple, CO 193 sts.
- Knit 1 row. Change to White.
- The outermost 3 sts at each side are edge sts and always knitted on every row. The pattern is worked over the center 187 sts between edge sts.
- Work in pattern until blanket measures approx. 32¾ in / 83 cm in length. End with a complete pattern repeat.
- BO loosely.
- With Light Purple, crochet edging all around blanket.
- Weave in all ends neatly on WS.
- Block by patting blanket to finished measurements on a damp towel. Place another damp towel on top and leave until completely dry.

□ = knit on RS, purl on WS
x = purl on RS, knit on WS
o = yo
/ = k2tog

FINISHED MEASUREMENTS
Approx. 27½ x 33 in / 70 x 84 cm

MATERIALS
Yarn:
CYCA #1 (fingering) Viking Garn Baby Ull (100% Merino wool, 191 yd/175 m / 50 g)
Yarn Color and Amount:
White 300: 350 g
Needles:
U. S. size 2.5 / 3 mm: 32 in / 80 cm circular; cable needle
Crochet Hook:
U. S. size B-1/C-2 / 2.5 mm for edging

STITCHES AND TECHNIQUES
Pattern
See chart.

Crocheted Edging
1 sc, *ch 2, 1 dc in same st as sc, skip ⅜ in / 1 cm, 1 sc in next st*; rep * to * around.

- The blanket is worked back and forth on a circular needle.
- CO 199 sts.
- The outermost st at each side is an edge st and always knitted. The first row = WS.
- Begin on WS with purl 1 row.
- Work in charted pattern until blanket measures approx. 31½ in / 80 cm in length. End with a complete pattern repeat.
- BO loosely.
- Crochet edging all around blanket.
- Weave in all ends neatly on WS.
- Block by gently steam pressing on WS under a damp pressing cloth.

□ = knit on RS, purl on WS
x = purl on RS, knit on WS
------> = place 3 sts on cable needle and hold behind work, k3, k3 from cable needle
<------ = place 3 sts on cable needle and hold in front of work, k3, k3 from cable needle

Chart follows.

repeat

Vilde

FINISHED MEASUREMENTS
Approx. 30¾ x 37½ in / 78 x 95 cm

MATERIALS
Yarn:
CYCA #1 (fingering) Viking Garn Baby Ull (100% Merino wool, 191 yd/175 m / 50 g)
Yarn Colors and Amounts:
White 300: 200 g
Yellow 342: 150 g
Needles:
U. S. size 6 / 4 mm: 32 in / 80 cm circular
The blanket is intentionally worked on a large needle, so it will be light and airy.
Crochet Hook:
U. S. size B-1/C-2 / 2.5 mm for edging

- The blanket is worked back and forth on a circular needle.
- With Yellow, CO 148 sts.
- Knit 22 ridges (= knit 44 rows).
- Knit 20 sts with Yellow. Change to White and work charted pattern over next 108 sts. Change to Yellow (using a second ball) and knit rem 20 sts.
- Throughout, work 20 sts at each side in garter st with Yellow and then, with White, work the center 108 sts in pattern between edge sts. At each color change, twist the strands around each other to avoid holes.
- Continue in pattern until blanket measures approx. 32¼ in / 82 cm in length. End with a complete pattern repeat.
- With Yellow, knit 22 ridges (= knit 44 rows).
- BO loosely.
- With White, crochet edging all around blanket.
- Weave in all ends neatly on WS.
- Block by patting out blanket to finished measurements and gently steam pressing on WS under a damp pressing cloth.

STITCHES AND TECHNIQUES
Garter Stitch
Knit back and forth on circular needle. Knit all rows. 2 rows = 1 ridge.

Pattern
See chart.

Crocheted Edging
Rnd 1: Work sc all around edge, with 3 sc in each corner st.
Rnd 2: 1 sc, *ch 2, 1 dc in same st as sc, skip 1 st, 1 sc in next st*; rep * to * around.

☐ = knit on RS, purl on WS
x = purl on RS, knit on WS

			x	x	x	
			x	x	x	
			x	x	x	
			x	x	x	
x	x	x				
x	x	x				
x	x	x				
x	x	x				

Dag

FINISHED MEASUREMENTS
Approx. 28¼ x 33½ in /
72 x 85 cm

MATERIALS
Yarn:
CYCA #1 (fingering) Viking
Garn Baby Ull (100% Merino
wool, 191 yd/175 m / 50 g)
Yarn Colors and Amounts:
Natural White 302: 100 g
Beige 307: 200 g
Needles:
U. S. size 6 / 4 mm: 32 in / 80 cm
circular
The blanket is intentionally
worked on a large needle, so it will
be light and airy.
Crochet Hook:
U. S. size B-1/C-2 / 2.5 mm for
edging

STITCHES AND TECHNIQUES
Garter Stitch
Knit back and forth on circular needle. Knit all rows. 2 rows =
1 ridge.

Pattern
See chart.

Crocheted Edging
Rnd 1: Work sc all around edge, with 3 sc in each corner st.
Rnd 2: 1 sc, *ch 2, 1 dc in same st as sc, skip 1 st, 1 sc in next st*;
rep * to * around.

- The blanket is worked back and forth on a circular needle.
- With Beige, CO 144 sts.
- Work in Pattern 1 for 4 in / 10 cm.
- Work 18 sts in Pattern 1 with Beige. Change to Natural White
  and work Pattern 2 over next 108 sts. Change to Beige (using
  a second ball) and work rem 18 sts in Pattern 1. At each color
  change, twist the strands around each other to avoid holes.
- Continue as est until Pattern 2 measures 8 blocks in length.
- Work 18 sts in Pattern 1 with Beige. Change to Natural White
  and work 24 sts in Pattern 2; with Beige, work 60 sts in Pattern
  3; with a new ball of Natural White, work 24 sts Pattern 2; end
  with 18 sts in Pattern 1 with Beige.
- Continue as est until Pattern 3 measures 17 blocks in length.
- With Beige, work 18 sts in Pattern 1. Change to Natural White
  and work Pattern 2 over next 108 sts. Change to Beige and
  work rem 18 sts in Pattern 1.
- Continue as est until Pattern 2 measures 8 blocks in length.
- With Beige, work in Pattern 1 for 4 in / 10 cm.
- BO loosely.
- With Natural White, crochet edging all around blanket.
- Weave in all ends neatly on WS.
- Block by patting out blanket to finished measurements and
  gently steam pressing on WS under a damp pressing cloth.

= knit on RS, purl on WS

	X
X	

= purl on RS, knit on WS

Chart—Pattern 1
Beige

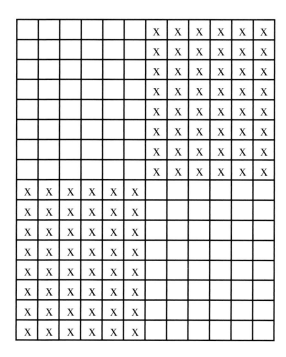

Chart—Pattern 3
Beige

Chart—Pattern 2
Natural White

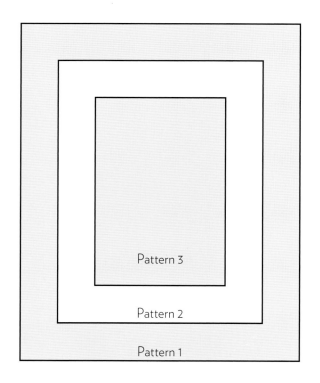

Pattern 3

Pattern 2

Pattern 1

Kaja

FINISHED MEASUREMENTS
Approx. 30¾ x 35 in / 78 x 89 cm

MATERIALS
Yarn:
CYCA #1 (fingering) Viking Garn Baby Ull (100% Merino wool, 191 yd/175 m / 50 g)
Yarn Colors and Amounts:
Natural White 302: 250 g
Beige 307: 100 g
Needles:
U. S. size 4 / 3.5 mm: 32 in / 80 cm circular
Crochet Hook:
U. S. size B-1/C-2 / 2.5 mm for edging

STITCHES AND TECHNIQUES
Garter Stitch
Knit back and forth on circular needle. Knit all rows. 2 rows = 1 ridge.

Pattern
See chart.

Crocheted Edging
Rnd 1: Work sc all around edge, with 3 sc in each corner st.
Rnd 2: 1 sc, *ch 2, 1 dc in same st as sc, skip 1 st, 1 sc in next st*; rep * to * around.

- The blanket is worked back and forth on a circular needle.
- With Natural White, CO 158 sts.
- Knit 1 row. Change to Beige and begin charted pattern.
- The outermost st at each side is an edge st and always knitted. The pattern is worked over the 156 sts between the edge sts.
- Continue as est until blanket measures approx. 34¾ in / 88 cm in length. End with a complete pattern repeat.
- With Beige, knit 1 ridge (= knit 2 rows) and then knit 1 ridge with Natural White.
- BO loosely.
- With Natural White, crochet edging all around blanket.
- Weave in all ends neatly on WS.
- Block by patting out blanket to finished measurements and gently steam pressing on WS under a damp pressing cloth.

☐ = knit on RS, purl on WS
x = purl on RS, knit on WS
o = yo
\ = sl 1, k1, psso (or ssk)

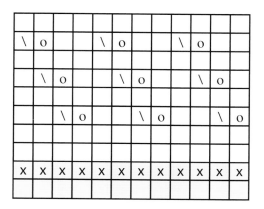

FINISHED MEASUREMENTS
Approx. 35 x 29½ in / 89 x 75 cm

MATERIALS
Yarn:
CYCA #1 (fingering) Viking Garn Baby Ull (100% Merino wool, 191 yd/175 m / 50 g)
Yarn Colors and Amounts:
Natural White 302: 150 g
Beige 307: 100 g
Brown 308: 100 g
Needles:
U. S. size 6 / 4 mm: 32 in / 80 cm circular
The blanket is intentionally worked on a large needle, so it will be light and airy.
Crochet Hook:
U. S. size D-3 / 3 mm for edging

STITCHES AND TECHNIQUES
Garter Stitch
Knit back and forth on circular needle. Knit all rows. 2 rows = 1 ridge.

Pattern
Knit 1 ridge (= knit 2 rows) Natural White, knit 1 ridge Beige, knit 1 ridge Brown; rep * to *.

Crocheted Edging
Rnd 1: Work sc all around edge, with 3 sc in each corner st.
Rnd 2: 1 sc, *ch 2, 2 dc in same st as sc, skip 1 sc, 1 sc in next st*; rep * to * around.

- The blanket is worked back and forth on a circular needle.
- With Natural White, CO 165 sts. Knit 1 row. You now have 1 ridge Natural White.
- Change to Beige and knit 1 ridge (= knit 2 rows). Next, change to Brown and knit 1 ridge.
- Rep garter stripe sequence until blanket measures approx. 28¼ in / 72 cm.
- End with a Natural White ridge.
- BO loosely.
- With Natural White, crochet edging all around blanket.
- Weave in all ends neatly on WS.
- Block by patting out blanket to finished measurements and gently steam pressing on WS under a damp pressing cloth.

Bjorn

FINISHED MEASUREMENTS
Approx. 29¼ x 37 in / 74 x 94 cm

MATERIALS
Yarn:
CYCA #1 (fingering) Viking Garn Baby Ull (100% Merino wool, 191 yd/175 m / 50 g)
Yarn Color and Amount:
Beige 307: 300 g
Needles:
U. S. size 6 / 4 mm: 32 in / 80 cm circular
The blanket is intentionally worked on a large needle, so it will be light and airy.

STITCHES AND TECHNIQUES
Garter Stitch
Knit back and forth on circular needle. Knit all rows. 2 rows = 1 ridge.

Pattern
See charts.

- The blanket is worked back and forth on a circular needle.
- CO 156 sts. Knit 1 row.
- Always begin each row with sl 1 knitwise.
- Knit 6 ridges (= knit 12 rows).
- The outermost 6 sts at each side are edge sts and always knitted. The pattern is worked over the center 144 sts between edge sts.
- Work in Pattern 1 for 6 in / 15 cm. End with a complete repeat. Work Pattern 3 once.
- Work in Pattern 2 for 6¾ in / 17 cm. Work Pattern 3 once.
- Work in Pattern 4 for 7 in / 18 cm. Work Pattern 3 once.
- Work in Pattern 2 for 6¾ in / 17 cm. Work Pattern 3 once.
- Work in Pattern 1 for 6 in / 15 cm. End with a complete repeat.
- Finish with knit 6 ridges (= knit 12 rows).
- BO loosely.
- Weave in all ends neatly on WS.
- Block by patting out blanket to finished measurements and gently steam pressing on WS under a damp pressing cloth.

□ = knit on RS, purl on WS

X = purl on RS, knit on WS

Chart—Pattern 1

1	2	3	4	5	6	7	8	9	10	11	12
						X	X	X	X	X	X
						X	X	X	X	X	X
						X	X	X	X	X	X
						X	X	X	X	X	X
						X	X	X	X	X	X
						X	X	X	X	X	X
						X	X	X	X	X	X
						X	X	X	X	X	X
X	X	X	X	X	X						
X	X	X	X	X	X						
X	X	X	X	X	X						
X	X	X	X	X	X						
X	X	X	X	X	X						
X	X	X	X	X	X						
X	X	X	X	X	X						
X	X	X	X	X	X						

Chart—Pattern 2

1	2	3	4	5	6
X				X	X
X				X	X
			X	X	X
			X	X	X
		X	X	X	
		X	X	X	
	X	X	X		
	X	X	X		
X	X	X			
X	X	X			

Chart—Pattern 3

1	2	3	4	5	6
X	X	X	X	X	X
X	X	X	X	X	X
X	X	X	X	X	X

Chart—Pattern 4

1	2	3	4
		X	X
		X	X
X	X		
X	X		

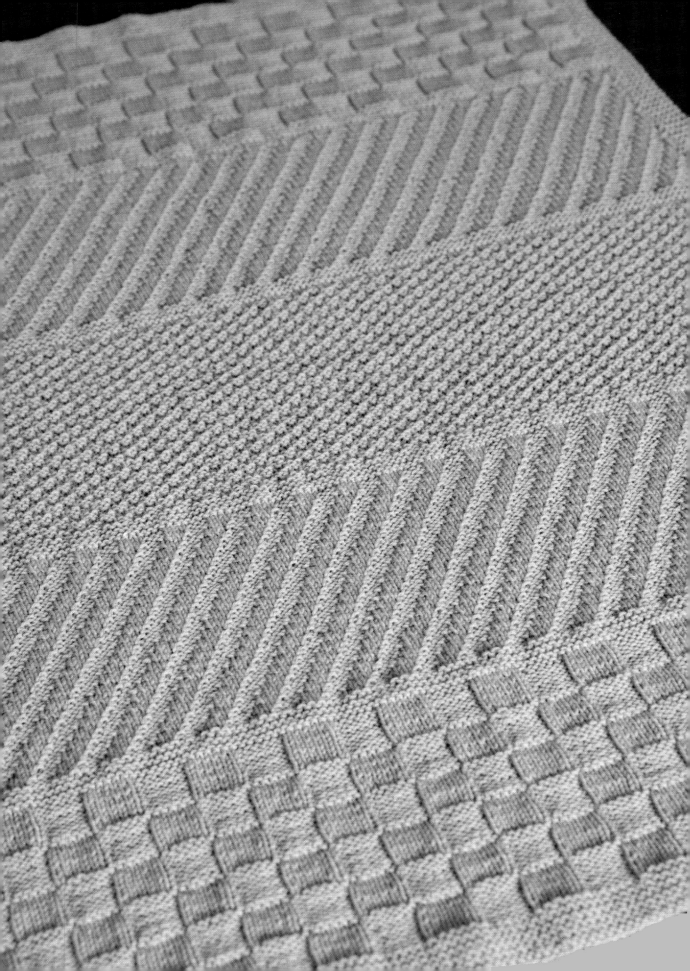

FINISHED MEASUREMENTS
Approx. 29¼ x 37 in / 74 x 94 cm

MATERIALS
Yarn:
CYCA #1 (fingering) Viking Garn Baby Ull (100% Merino wool, 191 yd/175 m / 50 g)
Yarn Color and Amount:
Light Purple 377: 300 g
Needles:
U. S. size 6 / 4 mm: 32 in / 80 cm circular
The blanket is intentionally worked on a large needle, so it will be light and airy.

STITCHES AND TECHNIQUES
Garter Stitch
Knit back and forth on circular needle. Knit all rows. 2 rows = 1 ridge.

Pattern
See charts. The pattern consists of large and small blocks.

- The blanket is worked back and forth on a circular needle.
- CO 156 sts.
- Always begin each row with sl 1 knitwise.
- Knit 6 ridges (= knit 12 rows).
- The outermost 6 sts at each side are edge sts and always knitted. The pattern is worked over the center 144 sts between edge sts. (See photo for arrangement of blocks.)
- Work in Pattern 1 over the first 24 sts (inside edge sts). Work in Pattern 2 over the next 24 sts. Continue, alternating large and small block patterns as est until there are 5 large blocks (Pattern 1) in length.
- Now work in Pattern 2 over the first 24 sts and Pattern 1 over the next 24 sts. Continue, alternating large and small block patterns as est until there are 5 large blocks (Pattern 1) in length.
- Repeat this sequence until there are 7 large block patterns (5 large blocks = 1 large block pattern) in length. The blanket should now measure approx. 36¼ in / 92 cm.
- Finish with knit 6 ridges (= knit 12 rows).
- BO loosely.
- Weave in all ends neatly on WS.
- Block by patting out blanket to finished measurements and gently steam pressing on WS under a damp pressing cloth.

☐ = knit on RS, purl on WS
X = purl on RS, knit on WS

Chart—Pattern 2

Chart—Pattern 1

Sindre

FINISHED MEASUREMENTS
Approx. 27¼ x 34¼ in /
69 x 87 cm

MATERIALS
Yarn:
CYCA #1 (fingering) Viking
Garn Baby Ull (100% Merino
wool, 191 yd/175 m / 50 g)
Yarn Color and Amount:
Light Blue 320: 250 g
Needles:
U. S. size 6 / 4 mm: 32 in / 80 cm
circular
The blanket is intentionally
worked on a large needle, so it will
be light and airy.

STITCHES AND TECHNIQUES
Garter Stitch
Knit back and forth on circular
needle. Knit all rows. 2 rows = 1
ridge.

Pattern
See chart.

- The blanket is worked back and forth on a circular needle.
- CO 156 sts.
- Always begin each row with sl 1 knitwise.
- Knit 6 ridges (= knit 12 rows).
- The outermost 6 sts at each side are edge sts and always knitted. The pattern is worked over the center 144 sts between edge sts.
- Work in charted pattern until blanket measures approx. 33½ in / 85 cm in length. End with a complete pattern repeat.
- Finish with 6 ridges (= knit 12 rows).
- BO loosely.
- Weave in all ends neatly on WS.
- Block by patting out blanket to finished measurements and gently steam pressing on WS under a damp pressing cloth.

☐ = knit on RS, purl on WS
ⵝ = purl on RS, knit on WS

						X	X	X	X	X	X
						X	X	X	X	X	X
						X	X	X	X	X	X
						X	X	X	X	X	X
						X	X	X	X	X	X
						X	X	X	X	X	X
X	X	X	X	X	X						
X	X	X	X	X	X						
X	X	X	X	X	X						
X	X	X	X	X	X						
X	X	X	X	X	X						
X	X	X	X	X	X						

FINISHED MEASUREMENTS

Approx. 29½ x 36¾ in /
75 x 93 cm

MATERIALS

Yarn:

CYCA #1 (fingering) Viking
Garn Baby Ull (100% Merino
wool, 191 yd/175 m / 50 g)

Yarn Color and Amount:

Mint Green 327: 300 g

Needles:

U. S. size 6 / 4 mm: 32 in / 80 cm
circular

The blanket is intentionally
worked on a large needle, so it will
be light and airy.

NOTE: The pattern will draw
the fabric in as you knit it. You
can stretch it out to finished
measurements when blocking.

STITCHES AND TECHNIQUES

Garter Stitch

Knit back and forth on circular
needle. Knit all rows. 2 rows = 1
ridge.

Pattern

See chart.

- The blanket is worked back and forth on a circular needle.
- CO 160 sts.
- Always begin each row with sl 1 knitwise.
- Knit 10 ridges (= knit 20 rows).
- The outermost 10 sts at each side are edge sts and always knitted. The pattern is worked over the center 140 sts between edge sts.
- Work in charted pattern until blanket measures approx. 35½ in / 90 cm in length. End with a complete pattern repeat.
- Finish with 10 ridges (= knit 20 rows).
- BO loosely.
- Weave in all ends neatly on WS.
- Block by patting out blanket to finished measurements and gently steam pressing on WS under a damp pressing cloth.

☐ = knit on RS, purl on WS
X = purl on RS, knit on WS

Maud

FINISHED MEASUREMENTS
Approx. 27¼ x 35 in / 69 x 89 cm

MATERIALS
Yarn:
CYCA #1 (fingering) Viking Garn Baby Ull (100% Merino wool, 191 yd/175 m / 50 g)
Yarn Color and Amount:
White 300: 300 g
Needles:
U. S. size 6 / 4 mm: 32 in / 80 cm circular
The blanket is intentionally worked on a large needle, so it will be light and airy.

STITCHES AND TECHNIQUES
Garter Stitch
Knit back and forth on circular needle. Knit all rows. 2 rows = 1 ridge.

Stockinette Stitch
Knit on RS and purl on WS.

Pattern
Rows 1-14: *K7 (garter st), 3 sts stockinette st*; rep * to * across, ending with k7 (garter).
Rows 15-28: K7 (garter st), *k7 (garter st), 3 sts stockinette st*; rep * to * across, ending with k14 (garter).
Rep Rows 1-28.

- The blanket is worked back and forth on a circular needle.
- CO 147 sts.
- Always begin each row with sl 1 knitwise.
- Knit 7 ridges (= knit 14 rows).
- Work in pattern until blanket measures approx. 33½ in / 85 cm in length. End with Rows 1-14.
- Finish with knit 7 ridges (= knit 14 rows).
- BO loosely.
- Weave in all ends neatly on WS.
- Block by patting out blanket to finished measurements and gently steam pressing on WS under a damp pressing cloth.

FINISHED MEASUREMENTS
Approx. 29¼ x 36¾ in /
74 x 93 cm

MATERIALS
Yarn:
CYCA #1 (fingering) Viking
Garn Baby Ull (100% Merino
wool, 191 yd/175 m / 50 g)
Yarn Color and Amount:
Old Rose 362: 300 g
Needles:
U. S. size 6 / 4 mm: 32 in / 80 cm
circular
The blanket is intentionally
worked on a large needle, so it will
be light and airy.

STITCHES AND TECHNIQUES
Garter Stitch
Knit back and forth on circular
needle. Knit all rows. 2 rows = 1
ridge.

Pattern
See chart.

- The blanket is worked back and forth on a circular needle.
- CO 174 sts.
- Always begin each row with sl 1 knitwise.
- Knit 6 ridges (= knit 12 rows).
- The outermost 6 sts at each side are edge sts and always knitted. The pattern is worked over the center 162 sts between edge sts.
- Work in charted pattern until blanket measures approx. 36 in / 91 cm in length. End with a complete pattern repeat.
- Finish with knit 6 ridges (= knit 12 rows).
- BO loosely.
- Weave in all ends neatly on WS.
- Block by patting out blanket to finished measurements and gently steam pressing on WS under a damp pressing cloth.

☐ = knit on RS, purl on WS
x = purl on RS, knit on WS

X					X
X					X
				X	X
				X	X
			X	X	
			X	X	
		X	X		
		X	X		
	X	X			
	X	X			
X	X				
X	X				

FINISHED MEASUREMENTS

Approx. 29¼ x 36¼ in / 74 x 92 cm

MATERIALS

Yarn:

CYCA #1 (fingering) Viking Garn Baby Ull (100% Merino wool, 191 yd/175 m / 50 g)

Yarn Color and Amount:

White 300: 350 g

Needles:

U. S. size 6 / 4 mm: 32 in / 80 cm circular

The blanket is intentionally worked on a large needle, so it will be light and airy.

Crochet Hook:

U. S. size B-1/C-2 / 2.5 mm for edging

STITCHES AND TECHNIQUES

Garter Stitch

Knit back and forth on circular needle. Knit all rows. 2 rows = 1 ridge.

Pattern

See chart.

Crocheted Edging

1 sc, *ch 2, 1 dc in same ridge/st as sc, skip 1 ridge/st, 1 sc in next ridge/st*; rep * to * around.

- The blanket is worked back and forth on a circular needle.
- CO 193 sts.
- Knit 3 ridges (= knit 6 rows).
- The outermost 3 sts at each side are edge sts and always knitted. The pattern is worked over the center 187 sts between edge sts.
- Work in charted pattern until blanket measures approx. 35½ in / 90 cm in length. End with a complete pattern repeat.
- Finish with 1 more ridge (= knit 2 more rows).
- BO loosely.
- Crochet edging all around blanket.
- Weave in all ends neatly on WS.
- Block by patting out blanket to finished measurements and gently steam pressing on WS under a damp pressing cloth.

	= knit on RS, purl on WS
x	= purl on RS, knit on WS
o	= yo
/	= k2tog

x	x	x	x	x	x	x	x	x	x	x	x	x	x	x	x	x	x
x	x	x	x	x	x	x	x	x	x	x	x	x	x	x	x	x	x
/	/	/	o		o		o		o		o		o		/	/	/

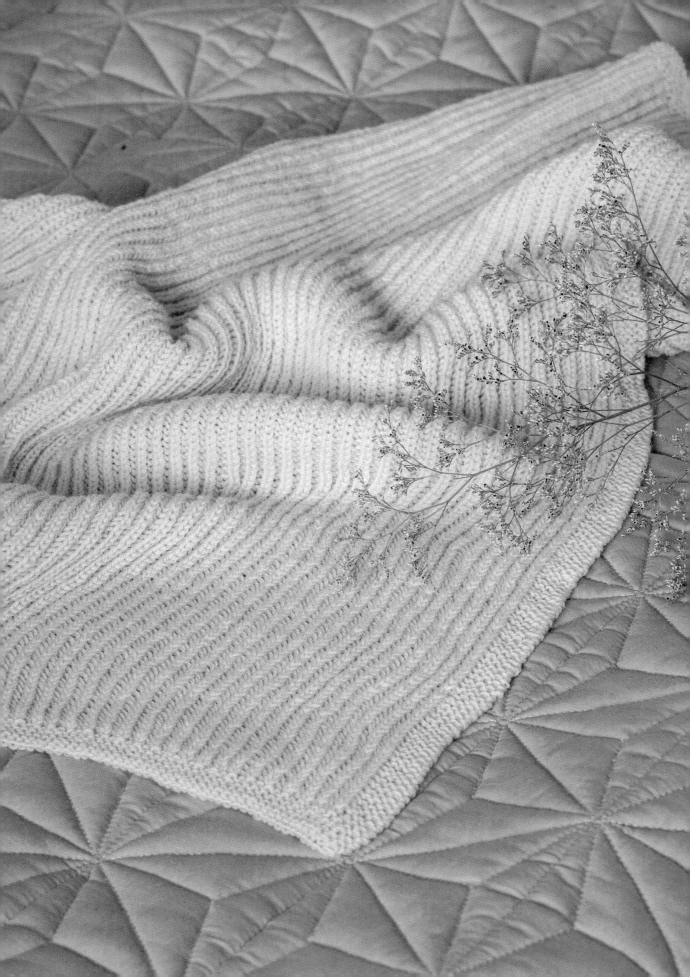

Jannicke

FINISHED MEASUREMENTS
Approx. 29½ x 36 in / 75 x 91 cm

MATERIALS
Yarn:
CYCA #1 (fingering) Dale Garn Baby Ull (100% Merino wool, 180 yd/165 m / 50 g)
Yarn Color and Amount:
Soft Yellow 2235: 400 g
Needles:
U. S. size 4 / 3.5 mm: 32 in / 80 cm circular
The blanket is intentionally worked on a large needle, so it will be light and airy.

STITCHES AND TECHNIQUES
Garter Stitch
Knit back and forth on circular needle. Knit all rows. 2 rows = 1 ridge.

Pattern
Row 1: (K1, p1) across.
Row 2: *Insert right needle through st of previous row, k1, and slip both sts off needle, p1*; rep * to * across.
Rep Rows 1-2.

- The blanket is worked back and forth on a circular needle.
- CO 150 sts.
- Always begin each row with sl 1 knitwise.
- Knit 4 ridges (= knit 8 rows).
- The outermost 4 sts at each side are edge sts and always knitted. The pattern is worked over the center 142 sts between edge sts.
- Work in pattern until blanket measures approx. 35 in / 89 cm in length.
- Finish with knit 4 ridges (= knit 8 rows).
- BO loosely.
- Weave in all ends neatly on WS.
- Block by patting out blanket to finished measurements and gently steam pressing on WS under a damp pressing cloth.

Petter

FINISHED MEASUREMENTS
Approx. 30¾ x 35½ in /
78 x 90 cm

MATERIALS
Yarn:
CYCA #1 (fingering) Viking Garn
Baby Ull (100% Merino wool, 191
yd/175 m / 50 g)
Yarn Color and Amount:
Pearl Gray 312: 400 g
Needles:
U. S. size 4 / 3.5 mm: 32 in / 80 cm
circular

STITCHES AND TECHNIQUES
Garter Stitch
Knit back and forth on circular
needle. Knit all rows. 2 rows = 1
ridge.

Pattern
See chart.

Stripe Pattern
Knit 8 ridges (= knit 16 rows).
Work Pattern 1; knit 8 ridges; work
Pattern 2.

- The blanket is worked back and forth on a circular needle.
- CO 168 sts.
- Always begin each row with sl 1 knitwise.
- Knit 8 ridges (= knit 16 rows).
- The outermost 8 sts at each side are edge sts and always knitted. The pattern is worked over the center 152 sts between edge sts.
- Work in pattern until blanket measures approx. 34¼ in / 87 cm in length. End with a complete pattern repeat.
- Pattern 1 is worked 9 times.
- Finish with knit 8 ridges (= knit 16 rows).
- BO loosely.
- Weave in all ends neatly on WS.
- Block by patting out blanket to finished measurements and gently steam pressing on WS under a damp pressing cloth.

☐ = knit on RS, purl on WS
/ = k2tog
\ = sl 1, k1, psso (or ssk)
o = yo

Pattern 1

Pattern 2

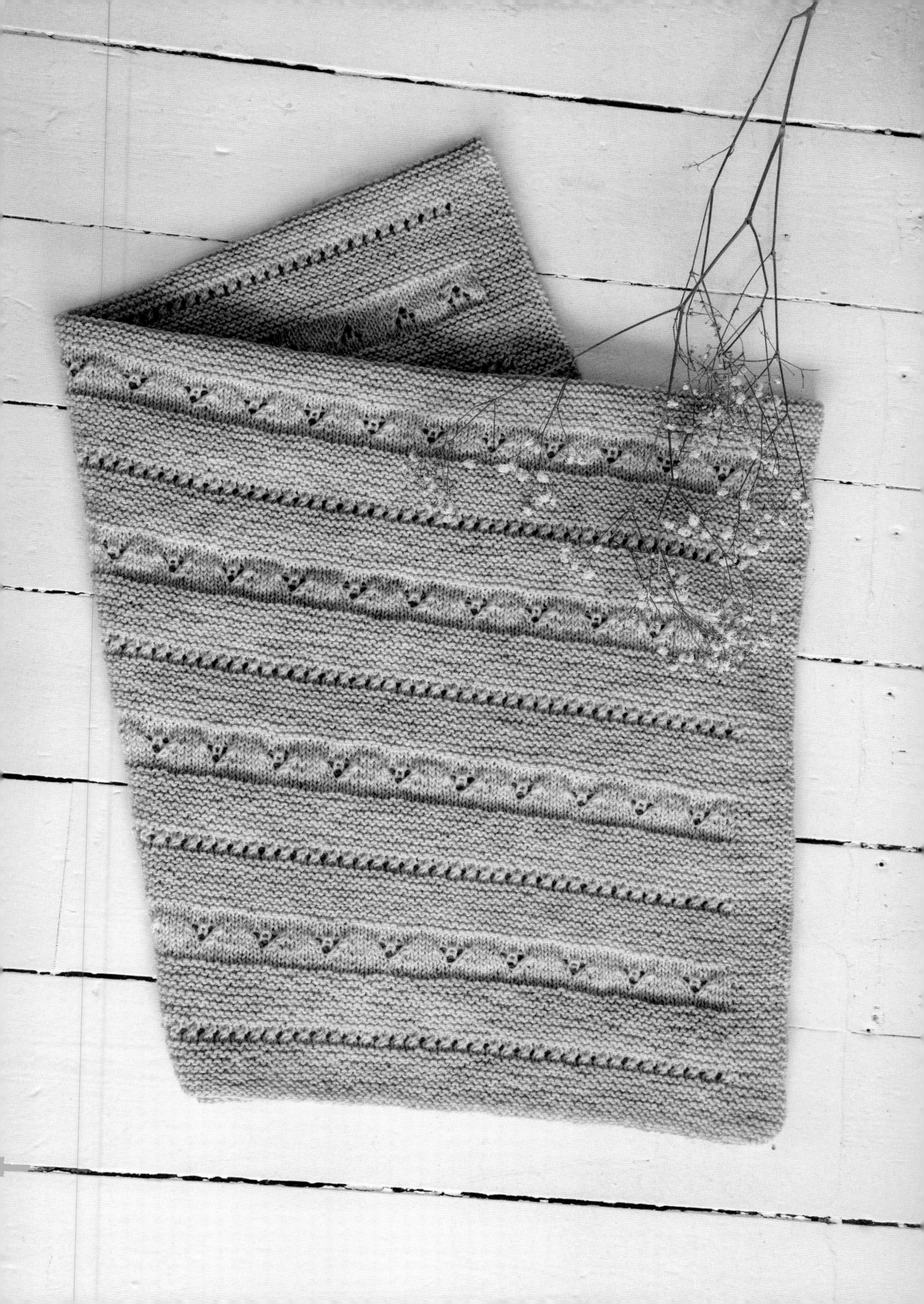

FINISHED MEASUREMENTS
Approx. 32 x 34¼ in / 81 x 87 cm

MATERIALS
Yarn:
CYCA #1 (fingering) Viking Garn Baby Ull (100% Merino wool, 191 yd/175 m / 50 g)
Yarn Color and Amount:
Light Pink 364: 350 g
Needles:
U. S. size 4 / 3.5 mm: 32 in / 80 cm circular

STITCHES AND TECHNIQUES
Garter Stitch
Knit back and forth on circular needle. Knit all rows. 2 rows = 1 ridge.

Pattern
See chart.

- The blanket is worked back and forth on a circular needle.
- CO 171 sts.
- Always begin each row with sl 1 knitwise.
- Knit 10 ridges (= knit 20 rows).
- The outermost 10 sts at each side are edge sts and always knitted. The pattern is worked over the center 151 sts between edge sts.
- Work in pattern until blanket measures approx. 33½ in / 85 cm in length. End with a complete pattern repeat.
- Finish with 5 ridges (= knit 10 rows). Including the last 5 ridges of pattern, there are now 10 ridges at top of blanket.
- BO loosely.
- Weave in all ends neatly on WS.
- Block by patting out blanket to finished measurements and gently steam pressing on WS under a damp pressing cloth.

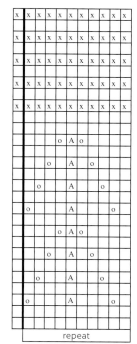

☐ = knit on RS, purl on WS
x = purl on RS, knit on WS
o = yo
A = sl 1, k1, psso (or ssk)

Nina

FINISHED MEASUREMENTS
Approx. 36 x 36 in / 91 x 91 cm

MATERIALS
Yarn:
CYCA #1 (fingering) Viking Garn Baby Ull (100% Merino wool, 191 yd/175 m / 50 g)
Yarn Colors and Amounts:
White 300: 150 g
Light Pink 364: 150 g
Old Rose 362: 150 g
Needles:
U. S. size 6 / 4 mm: 32 in / 80 cm circular
The blanket is intentionally worked on a large needle, so it will be light and airy.
Crochet Hook:
U. S. size B-1/C-2 / 2.5 mm for edging

STITCHES AND TECHNIQUES
Garter Stitch
Knit back and forth on circular needle. Knit all rows. 2 rows = 1 ridge.

Pattern
Row 1: Knit to center st, yo, k1 (center st), yo, knit to end of row.
Row 2: Knit, working all yarnovers as k1 tbl.
Rep Rows 1-2 (2 knit rows = 1 ridge).

Color Stripe Sequence
Alternate knitting 3 ridges of each color in the sequence: Old Rose, Light Pink, White.

Crocheted Edging
Rnd 1: Work sc all around edge, with 3 sc in each corner st.
Rnd 2: 1 sc, *ch 2, 1 dc in same st as sc, skip 1 sc, 1 sc in next st*; rep * to * around.

- The blanket is worked back and forth on a circular needle.
- With Old Rose, CO 3 sts.
- K3; pm in the center st.
- Work pattern in color stripe sequence until blanket measures approx. 35 x 35 in / 89 x 89 cm.
- End pattern after 3 White ridges.
- BO loosely with Old Rose.
- With Old Rose, crochet edging all around blanket.
- Weave in all ends neatly on WS.
- Block by patting out blanket to finished measurements and gently steam pressing on WS under a damp pressing cloth.

FINISHED MEASUREMENTS
Approx. 32¼ x 36¾ in / 82 x 93 cm

MATERIALS
Yarn:
CYCA #1 (fingering) Viking Garn Baby Ull (100% Merino wool, 191 yd/175 m / 50 g)
Yarn Color and Amount:
Natural White 302: 350 g
Needles:
U. S. size 4 / 3.5 mm: 32 in / 80 cm circular
Crochet Hook:
U. S. size B-1/C-2 / 2.5 mm for edging

NOTE: The pattern draws the fabric in as you knit it. You can stretch it out to finished measurements when blocking.

STITCHES AND TECHNIQUES
Garter Stitch
Knit back and forth on circular needle. Knit all rows. 2 rows = 1 ridge.

Pattern
See chart.

Crocheted Edging
1 sc, *ch 2, 1 dc in same ridge/st as sc, skip 1 ridge/st, 1 sc in next ridge/st*; rep * to * around.

- The blanket is worked back and forth on a circular needle.
- CO 203 sts.
- Knit 5 ridges (= knit 10 rows).
- The outermost 5 sts at each side are edge sts and always knitted. The pattern is worked over the center 193 sts between edge sts.
- Work in pattern until blanket measures approx. 35 in / 89 cm in length. End with a complete pattern repeat.
- Finish with knit 5 ridges (= knit 10 rows).
- BO loosely.
- Crochet edging all around blanket.
- Weave in all ends neatly on WS.
- Block by patting out blanket to finished measurements and gently steam pressing on WS under a damp pressing cloth.

	= knit on RS, purl on WS
X	= purl on RS, knit on WS
o	= yo
<-------	= sl 1, k2, psso the two knit sts

X	X	X		o		X	X	X
X	X	X	<------			X	X	X
X	X	X				X	X	X
X	X	X				X	X	X
			repeat					

Bernhard

FINISHED MEASUREMENTS
Approx. 34¼ x 37½ in / 87 x 95 cm

MATERIALS
Yarn:
CYCA #1 (fingering) Viking Garn Baby Ull (100% Merino wool, 191 yd/175 m / 50 g)
Yarn Colors and Amounts:
White 300: 150 g
Light Blue 324: 150 g
Mint Green 327: 150 g
Needles:
U. S. size 4 / 3.5 mm: 32 in / 80 cm circular
Crochet Hook:
U. S. size B-1/C-2 / 2.5 mm for edging

STITCHES AND TECHNIQUES
Garter Stitch
Knit back and forth on circular needle. Knit all rows. 2 rows = 1 ridge.

Pattern
Alternate Blue and Green stripes following the chart. Knit 2 ridges (= 4 rows) in White between each stripe.

Crocheted Edging
Rnd 1: Work sc all around edge, with 3 sc in each corner st.
Rnd 2: 1 sc, *ch 2, 1 dc in same st as sc, skip 1 sc, 1 sc in next st*; rep * to * around.

- The blanket is worked back and forth on a circular needle.
- With White, CO 214 sts.
- The outermost st at each side is an edge st that is always knitted.
- Knit 3 rows.
- Change to Blue and begin charted pattern.
- Continue in pattern and stripes until blanket measures approx. 36¼ in / 92 cm in length. End with a complete pattern repeat + 2 ridges in White.
- BO loosely.
- With White, crochet edging all around blanket.
- Weave in all ends neatly on WS.
- Block by patting out blanket to finished measurements and gently steam pressing on WS under a damp pressing cloth.

□ = knit on RS, purl on WS
o = yo
A = sl 1, k2tog, psso

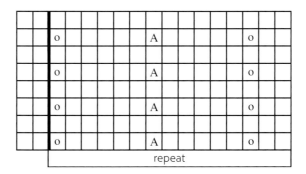

repeat

Sigrid

FINISHED MEASUREMENTS
Approx. 34 x 36 in / 86 x 91 cm

MATERIALS
Yarn:
CYCA #1 (fingering) Dale Garn
Baby Ull (100% Merino wool, 180
yd/165 m / 50 g)
Yarn Color and Amount:
Soft Yellow 2235: 350 g
Needles:
U. S. size 2.5 / 3 mm: 32 in / 80 cm
circular

STITCHES AND TECHNIQUES
Garter Stitch
Knit back and forth on circular
needle. Knit all rows. 2 rows = 1
ridge.

Pattern
See chart.

- The blanket is worked back and forth on a circular needle.
- CO 201 sts.
- Always begin each row with sl 1 knitwise.
- Knit 5 ridges (= knit 10 rows).
- The outermost 5 sts at each side are edge sts and always knitted. The pattern is worked over the center 191 sts between edge sts.
- Work in pattern until blanket measures approx. 33 in / 84 cm in length. End with a complete pattern repeat (or, if necessary, a half repeat).
- Finish with 5 ridges (= knit 10 rows).
- BO loosely.
- Weave in all ends neatly on WS.
- Block by patting out blanket to finished measurements and gently steam pressing on WS under a damp pressing cloth.

Chart key:
- ☐ = knit on RS, purl on WS
- X = purl on RS, knit on WS

	X	X	X	X	X	X	X	X	X	
	X	X	X	X	X	X	X	X	X	
		X	X	X	X	X	X	X		
		X	X	X	X	X	X	X		
			X	X	X	X	X			
			X	X	X	X	X			
				X	X	X				
				X	X	X				
					X					
					X					
	X	X	X	X		X	X	X	X	X
	X	X	X	X		X	X	X	X	X
X	X	X	X				X	X	X	X
X	X	X	X				X	X	X	X
X	X	X						X	X	X
X	X	X						X	X	X
X	X								X	X
X	X								X	X
X										X
X										X

repeat

Peder

FINISHED MEASUREMENTS
Approx. 34¼ x 37¾ in /
87 x 96 cm

MATERIALS
Yarn:
CYCA #1 (fingering) Sandnes
Garn Mini Alpakka (100% alpaca,
164 yd/150 m / 50 g)
Yarn Color and Amount:
Lilac 5031: 400 g
Needles:
U. S. size 2.5 / 3 mm: 32 in / 80 cm
circular

STITCHES AND TECHNIQUES
Garter Stitch
Knit back and forth on circular
needle. Knit all rows. 2 rows = 1
ridge.

Pattern
See chart.

- The blanket is worked back and forth on a circular needle.
- CO 186 sts.
- Always begin each row with sl 1 knitwise.
- Knit 6 ridges (= knit 12 rows).
- The outermost 5 sts at each side are edge sts and always knitted. The pattern is worked over the center 176 sts between edge sts.
- Work in pattern until blanket measures approx. 36¼ in / 92 cm in length. End with a complete pattern repeat.
- Finish with 6 ridges (= knit 12 rows).
- BO loosely.
- Weave in all ends neatly on WS.
- Block by patting out blanket to finished measurements and gently steam pressing on WS under a damp pressing cloth.

	= knit on RS, purl on WS
x	= purl on RS, knit on WS
o	= yo
\	= sl 1, k1, psso (or ssk)
/	= k2tog

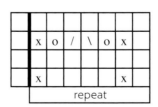

Torunn

FINISHED MEASUREMENTS
Approx. 30¼ x 35½ in /
77 x 90 cm

MATERIALS
Yarn:
CYCA #1 (fingering) Viking
Garn Baby Ull (100% Merino
wool, 191 yd/175 m / 50 g)
Yarn Color and Amount:
White 300: 350 g
Needles:
U. S. size 4 / 3.5 mm: 32 in / 80
cm circular
Crochet Hook:
U. S. size B-1/C-2 / 2.5 mm for
edging

STITCHES AND TECHNIQUES
Seed Stitch
Row 1: *K1, p1*; rep * to * across.
Row 2: Work knit over purl and
purl over knit.
Rep Rows 1-2.

Pattern
See chart.

Crocheted Edging
1 sc, *ch 2, 1 dc in same st as sc,
skip 3/8 in / 1 cm, 1 sc in next st*;
rep * to * around.

- The blanket is worked back and forth on a circular needle.
- CO 192 sts.
- Work in seed st for 2½ in / 6 cm.
- The outermost 11 sts at each side are edge sts and always worked in seed st. The pattern is worked over the center 170 sts between edge sts.
- Continue in pattern until blanket measures approx. 32¾ in / 83 cm in length. End with a complete pattern repeat.
- Finish with 2½ in / 6 cm seed st.
- BO loosely.
- Crochet edging all around blanket.
- Weave in all ends neatly on WS.
- Block by patting out blanket to finished measurements and gently steam pressing on WS under a damp pressing cloth.

X											X
X		\		o							X
X											X
X			\		o						X
X											X
X				\		o					X
X											X
X					\		o				X
X											X
X						\		o			X
X											X
X					o		/				X
X											X
X				o		/					X
X											X
X			o		/						X
X											X
X		o		/							X
X											X
X	o		/								X

☐	= knit on RS, purl on WS
X	= purl on RS, knit on WS
/	= k2tog
\	= sl 1, k1, psso (or ssk)
o	= yo

FINISHED MEASUREMENTS

Approx. 30¾ x 35½ in /
78 x 90 cm

MATERIALS

Yarn:

CYCA #1 (fingering) Viking
Garn Baby Ull (100% Merino
wool, 191 yd/175 m / 50 g)

Yarn Color and Amount:

Mint Green 327: 350 g

Needles:

U. S. size 4 / 3.5 mm: 32 in /
80 cm circular

STITCHES AND TECHNIQUES

Garter Stitch

Knit back and forth on circular
needle. Knit all rows. 2 rows = 1
ridge.

Pattern

See chart.

- The blanket is worked back and forth on a circular needle.
- CO 192 sts.
- Always begin each row with sl 1 knitwise.
- Knit 6 ridges (= knit 12 rows).
- Next Row (WS): K6, p180, k6.
- The outermost 6 sts at each side are edge sts and always knitted. The pattern is worked over the center 180 sts between edge sts.
- Work pattern until blanket measures approx. 34¾ in / 88 cm in length. End with a complete pattern repeat.
- Finish with 6 ridges (= knit 12 rows).
- BO loosely.
- Weave in all ends neatly on WS.
- Block by patting out blanket to finished measurements and gently steam pressing on WS under a damp pressing cloth.

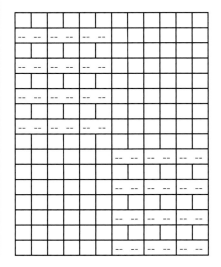

☐ = knit on RS, purl on WS

‗ ‗ = yo, k2, psso the
2 knit sts

Jens

FINISHED MEASUREMENTS
Approx. 32 x 37¾ in / 81 x 96 cm

MATERIALS
Yarn:
CYCA #1 (fingering) Viking
Garn Baby Ull (100% Merino
wool, 191 yd/175 m / 50 g)
Yarn Color and Amount:
Light Blue 324: 350 g
Needles:
U. S. size 4 / 3.5 mm: 32 in /
80 cm circular
Crochet Hook:
U. S. size B-1/C-2 / 2.5 mm for
edging

STITCHES AND TECHNIQUES
Pattern
See chart.

Crocheted Edging
1 sc, *ch 2, 1 dc in same st as sc,
skip 3/8 in / 1 cm, 1 sc in next st*;
rep * to * around.

- The blanket is worked back and forth on a circular needle.
- CO 190 sts.
- The outermost st at each side is an edge st and always knitted.
- Purl the first row = WS.
- Begin pattern following the chart.
- Work in pattern until blanket measures approx. 35 in / 89 cm in length. End with a complete stripe of the bamboo pattern.
- BO loosely.
- Crochet edging all around blanket.
- Weave in all ends neatly on WS.
- Block by patting out blanket to finished measurements and gently steam pressing on WS under a damp pressing cloth.

	= knit on RS, purl on WS
X	= purl on RS, knit on WS
-- --	= yo, k2, psso the 2 knit sts

Arna

FINISHED MEASUREMENTS
Approx. 36¼ x 36¾ in /
92 x 93 cm

MATERIALS
Yarn:
CYCA #1 (fingering) Gjestal
Merino Babyull (100% superwash
Merino wool, 191 yd/175 m / 50 g)
Yarn Colors and Amounts:
White 801: 350 g
Ice Pink 883: 300 g
Needles:
U. S. size 8 / 5 mm: 32 in / 80 cm
circular
The blanket is intentionally
worked on a large needle, so it will
be light and airy.
Crochet Hook:
U. S. size B-1/C-2 / 2.5 mm for
edging

STITCHES AND TECHNIQUES
Garter Stitch
Knit back and forth on circular
needle. Knit all rows. 2 rows = 1
ridge.

Crocheted Edging
1 sc, *ch 2, 2 dc in same ridge/
st as sc, skip 1 ridge/st, 1 sc in
next ridge/st*; rep from * to * all
around outer edge of blanket.

- The blanket is worked back and forth on a circular needle.
- With 1 strand of each color held together, CO 140 sts.
- Work in garter st (with both strands held together) until blanket measures approx. 36¼ in / 92 cm in length.
- BO loosely.
- With 1 strand of White, crochet edging all around blanket.
- Weave in all ends neatly on WS.
- Block by patting out blanket to finished measurements and gently steam pressing on WS under a damp pressing cloth.

Anne

FINISHED MEASUREMENTS
Approx. 26¾ x 34¼ in /
68 x 87 cm

MATERIALS
Yarn:
CYCA #3 (DK, light worsted)
Garnstudio Drops Baby Merino
Extra Fine (100% superwash
Merino wool, 115 yd/105 m / 50 g)
Yarn Color and Amount:
Light Yellow 24: 400 g
Needles:
U. S. size 6 / 4 mm: 32 in / 80 cm
circular

STITCHES AND TECHNIQUES
Seed Stitch
Row 1: *K1, p1*; rep * to * across.
Row 2: Work knit over purl and
purl over knit.
Rep Rows 1-2.

Pattern
See chart.

- The blanket is worked back and forth on a circular needle.
- CO 125 sts.
- Work in seed st for 12 rows.
- **Next Row (WS):** 7 sts in seed st, p111, 7 sts in seed st.
- The outermost 7 sts at each side are edge sts and always worked in seed st.
- The charted pattern is worked over the center 111 sts between edge sts.
- Continue in pattern until blanket measures approx. 32¼ in / 82 cm in length. End with a complete pattern repeat + Row 1 of chart.
- **Next Row (WS):** 7 sts in seed st, p111, 7 sts in seed st.
- Finish with 12 rows seed st.
- BO loosely.
- Weave in all ends neatly on WS.
- Block by patting out blanket to finished measurements and gently steam pressing on WS under a damp pressing cloth.

☐ = knit on RS, purl on WS

☒ = purl on RS, knit on WS

	X		X						X		X	
		X		X				X		X		
			X		X		X		X			
				X		X		X		X		
					X		X		X			
						X		X				
					X		X		X			
				X		X		X		X		
			X		X		X		X			
		X		X				X		X		
	X		X						X		X	
		X								X		

repeat

Ginger

FINISHED MEASUREMENTS
Approx. 25½ x 35½ in /
65 x 90 cm

MATERIALS
Yarn:
CYCA #3 (DK, light worsted)
Garnstudio Drops Baby Merino
Extra Fine (100% superwash
Merino wool, 115 yd/105 m / 50 g)
Yarn Color and Amount:
Pistachio 26: 400 g
Needles:
U. S. size 6 / 4 mm: 32 in / 80 cm
circular

STITCHES AND TECHNIQUES
Garter Stitch
Knit back and forth on circular
needle. Knit all rows. 2 rows = 1
ridge.

Pattern
See chart.

- The blanket is worked back and forth on a circular needle.
- CO 128 sts.
- Always begin each row with sl 1 knitwise.
- Knit 4 ridges (= knit 8 rows).
- The outermost 4 sts at each side are edge sts and always worked in garter st.
- The pattern is worked over the center 120 sts between edge sts.
- Continue in pattern until blanket measures approx. 34¼ in / 87 cm in length. End with a complete pattern repeat.
- Finish with 4 ridges (= knit 8 rows).
- BO loosely.
- Weave in all ends neatly on WS.
- Block by patting out blanket to finished measurements and gently steam pressing on WS under a damp pressing cloth.

☐ = knit on RS, purl on WS
☒ = purl on RS, knit on WS

						X	X	X	X	X	X
X							X	X	X	X	X
X	X							X	X	X	X
X	X	X							X	X	X
X	X	X	X							X	X
X	X	X	X	X							X
X	X	X	X	X	X						
						X	X	X	X	X	X
					X		X	X	X	X	X
			X	X			X	X	X	X	
		X	X	X					X	X	X
	X	X	X	X						X	X
X	X	X	X	X							X
X	X	X	X	X	X						

For the Littlest Ones

Some babies come into the world a little early, and are so small that they have to lie in an incubator at first. Premature babies are often small and thin, with fine, delicate skin. Both premature babies and full-term newborns need warmth, and an cozy little blanket will help. Knit with fine alpaca and silk yarn to make your blanket extra warm and soft; special baby wool yarn is also a good choice. When you're knitting blankets for the smallest babies, make sure to add in some extra love with every stitch.

FINISHED MEASUREMENTS
Approx. 15¾ x 19 in / 40 x 48 cm

MATERIALS
Yarn:
CYCA #2 (sport, baby)
Garnstudio Drops Baby Alpaca
Silk (70% baby alpaca, 30%
mulberry silk, 183 yd/167 m / 50 g)
Yarn Color and Amount:
White 1101: 100 g
Needles:
U. S. size 2.5 / 3 mm: 32 in / 80 cm
circular

- The blanket is worked back and forth on a circular needle.
- CO 112 sts.
- Always begin each row with sl 1 knitwise.
- Knit 5 ridges (= knit 10 rows).
- The outermost 5 sts at each side are edge sts and always worked in garter st. The charted pattern is worked over the center 102 sts between edge sts.
- Continue in pattern as est until blanket measures approx. 18¼ in / 46 cm in length. End with a complete pattern repeat.
- BO loosely.
- Finish with 5 ridges (= knit 10 rows).
- Weave in all ends neatly on WS.
- Block by patting out blanket to finished measurements and gently steam pressing on WS under a damp pressing cloth.

STITCHES AND TECHNIQUES
Garter Stitch
Knit back and forth on circular needle. Knit all rows. 2 rows = 1 ridge.

Pattern
See chart.

□ = knit on RS, purl on WS
X = purl on RS, knit on WS

Lykke

FINISHED MEASUREMENTS
Approx. 14¼ x 18½ in /
36 x 47 cm

MATERIALS
Yarn:
CYCA #2 (sport, baby)
Garnstudio Drops Baby Alpaca
Silk (70% baby alpaca, 30%
mulberry silk, 183 yd/167 m / 50 g)
Yarn Color and Amount:
White 1101: 150 g
Needles:
U. S. size 2.5 / 3 mm: 32 in / 80 cm
circular

NOTE: The pattern will
draw the fabric in, making the
blanket stretchy and soft. This is
deliberate; don't try to flatten it
out or steam press it.

STITCHES AND TECHNIQUES
Garter Stitch
Knit back and forth on circular
needle. Knit all rows. 2 rows = 1
ridge.

Pattern
See chart.

- The blanket is worked back and forth on a circular needle.
- CO 153 sts.
- Always begin each row with sl 1 knitwise.
- Knit 5 ridges (= knit 10 rows).
- The outermost 5 sts at each side are edge sts and always worked in garter st. The charted pattern is worked over the center 143 sts between edge sts.
- Continue in pattern as est until blanket measures approx. 18¼ in / 46 cm in length. End with a complete pattern repeat.
- BO loosely.
- Finish with 5 ridges (= knit 10 rows).
- Weave in all ends neatly on WS.
- Block by laying blanket between two damp towels until completely dry.

	= knit on RS, purl on WS
x	= purl on RS, knit on WS
o	= yo
<-------	= sl 1, k2, psso the 2 knit sts

		x	x		o		x	x			
		x	x	<------			x	x			
		x	x				x	x			
		x	x				x	x			
					repeat						

FINISHED MEASUREMENTS
Approx. 16½ x 20 in / 42 x 51 cm

MATERIALS
Yarn:
CYCA #2 (sport, baby)
Garnstudio Drops Baby Alpaca
Silk (70% baby alpaca, 30%
mulberry silk, 183 yd/167 m / 50 g)
Yarn Color and Amount:
Ice Blue 8112: 100 g
Needles:
U. S. size 2.5 / 3 mm: 32 in / 80 cm
circular

STITCHES AND TECHNIQUES
Garter Stitch
Knit back and forth on circular
needle. Knit all rows. 2 rows = 1
ridge.

Pattern
See chart.

- The blanket is worked back and forth on a circular needle.
- CO 104 sts.
- Always begin each row with sl 1 knitwise.
- Knit 5 ridges (= knit 10 rows).
- Knit 1 row on RS.
- **Next Row (WS):** K5, p94, k5.
- The outermost 5 sts at each side are edge sts and always worked in garter st. The charted pattern is worked over the center 94 sts between edge sts.
- Continue in pattern as est until blanket measures approx. 19¼ in / 49 cm in length. End with a complete pattern repeat.
- Finish with 5 ridges (= knit 10 rows).
- BO loosely.
- Weave in all ends neatly on WS.
- Block by laying blanket between two damp towels until completely dry.

☐ = knit on RS, purl on WS
o = yo
/ = k2tog
\ = sl 1, k2, psso (or ssk)

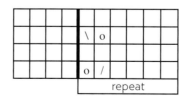

repeat

FINISHED MEASUREMENTS
Approx. 17 x 21 in / 43 x 53 cm

MATERIALS
Yarn:
CYCA #2 (sport, baby)
Garnstudio Drops Baby Alpaca
Silk (70% baby alpaca, 30%
mulberry silk, 183 yd/167 m / 50 g)
Yarn Color and Amount:
White 1101: 100 g
Needles:
U. S. size 2.5 / 3 mm: 32 in / 80 cm
circular
Crochet Hook:
U. S. size B-1/C-2 / 2.5 mm for
edging

STITCHES AND TECHNIQUES
Garter Stitch
Knit back and forth on circular
needle. Knit all rows. 2 rows = 1
ridge.

Pattern
See chart.

Crocheted Edging
1 sc, *ch 2, 1 dc in same st as sc,
skip ⅜ in / 1 cm, 1 sc in next st*;
rep from * to * all around outer
edge of blanket.

- The blanket is worked back and forth on a circular needle.
- CO 101 sts.
- Work in Pattern 1 until blanket is approx. 8¼ in / 21 cm long.
- Now work the first 38 sts in Pattern 1, next 25 sts in Pattern 2, and end with 38 sts in Pattern 1. The block with the heart should be centered on the blanket.
- After completing Pattern 2, work 8¼ in / 21 cm in Pattern 1 only.
- BO loosely.
- Crochet edging all around blanket.
- Weave in all ends neatly on WS.
- Block by laying blanket between two damp towels until completely dry.

	= knit on RS, purl on WS
x	= purl on RS, knit on WS
o	= yo
/	= k2tog
\	= sl 1, k2, psso (or ssk)
A	= sl 1, k2tog, psso

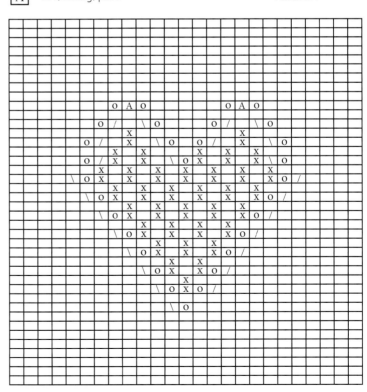

Pattern 1

Pattern 2

Cuddle Bags

A cuddle bag embraces a baby like a soft cocoon. It's both practical and cozy, a comfy choice for babies 0-3 months old—depending on how quickly they grow. A handmade cuddle bag is a wonderful gift for a newborn, and perfect in the baby carriage or crib.

Daniel

SIZE
0-3 months

MATERIALS
Yarn:
CYCA #1 (fingering) Gjestal
Merino Babyull (100% superwash
Merino wool, 191 yd/175 m / 50 g)
Yarn Colors and Amounts:
White 801: 150 g
Mint 886: 150 g
Needles:
U. S. size 7 / 4.5 mm: 24 in / 60
cm circular and set of 5 dpn
Crochet Hook:
U. S. size B-1/C-2 / 2.5 mm for
edging

STITCHES AND TECHNIQUES
Seed Stitch
Row 1: *K1, p1*; rep * to * across.
Row 2: Work knit over purl and
purl over knit.
Rep Rows 1-2.

Crocheted Edging
1 sc, *ch 2, 1 dc in same st as sc,
skip ⅜ in / 1 cm, 1 sc in next st*;
rep from * to * all around outer
edge of collar.

- With one strand of each color held together, CO 100 sts.
- Work back and forth in seed st for 6¾ in / 17 cm.
- Join to work in the round.
- Work *5 sts in seed st, k5*; rep from * to * around.
- Continue in pattern as est until cuddle bag is approx. 19¼ in / 49 cm long, including "collar."
- Begin decreases to shape cuddle bag, *at the same time* continuing in seed and stockinette st pattern. Change to dpn when sts no longer fit around circular.
  Decrease Rnd 1: *8 sts pattern, k2tog*; rep * to * around. Knit 1 rnd.
  Decrease Rnd 2: *7 sts pattern, k2tog*; rep * to * around. Knit 1 rnd.
  Decrease Rnd 3: *6 sts pattern, k2tog*; rep * to * around. Knit 1 rnd.
  Decrease Rnd 4: *5 sts pattern, k2tog*; rep * to * around. Knit 1 rnd.
  Decrease Rnd 5: *4 sts pattern, k2tog*; rep * to * around. Knit 1 rnd.
  Decrease Rnd 6: *3 sts pattern, k2tog*; rep * to * around. Knit 1 rnd.
  Decrease Rnd 7: *2 sts pattern, k2tog*; rep * to * around. Knit 1 rnd.
  Decrease Rnd 8: *K1, k2tog*; rep * to * around. Knit 1 rnd.
  Decrease Rnd 9: K2tog around = 10 sts rem. Knit 1 rnd.
- Cut yarn and draw end through rem sts; tighten.
- With 1 strand of White, beginning at center front, crochet edging all around "collar."
- Weave in all ends neatly on WS.
- Block by patting out cuddle bag to finished measurements and gently steam pressing on WS under a damp pressing cloth.

Elen

SIZE
0-3 months

MATERIALS
Yarn:
CYCA #1 (fingering) Viking Garn Baby Ull (100% Merino wool, 191 yd/175 m / 50 g)
Yarn Colors and Amounts:
White 300: 200 g
Needles:
U. S. size 4 / 3.5 mm: 24 in / 60 cm circular and set of 5 dpn
Crochet Hook:
U. S. size B-1/C-2 / 2.5 mm for edging

STITCHES AND TECHNIQUES
Seed Stitch
Row 1: *K1, p1*; rep * to * across.
Row 2: Work knit over purl and purl over knit.
Rep Rows 1-2.

Pattern
See chart.

Crocheted Edging
1 sc, *ch 2, 1 dc in same st as sc, skip 3/8 in / 1 cm, 1 sc in next st*; rep from * to * all around outer edge of collar.

- CO 150 sts.
- Work back and forth in seed st for 6¾ in / 17 cm.
- Pm when 26 sts rem on needle. This will now be the beginning of rnd. Continue, working in the round.
- The pattern at the center is worked over 51 sts.
- Work in pattern following chart; rep 3 times across center of cuddle bag. Knit rem sts of rnd.
- Continue in pattern as est until cuddle bag is approx. 19¼ in / 49 cm long, including "collar." End with a complete pattern repeat.
- Knit 1 rnd.
- Begin decreases to shape cuddle bag, at the same time continuing in seed and stockinette st pattern. Change to dpn when sts no longer fit around circular.
Decrease Rnd 1: *K8, k2tog*; rep * to * around.
Knit 1 rnd.
Decrease Rnd 2: *K7, k2tog*; rep * to * around.
Knit 1 rnd.
Decrease Rnd 3: *K6, k2tog*; rep * to * around.
Knit 1 rnd.
Decrease Rnd 4: *K5, k2tog*; rep * to * around.
Knit 1 rnd.
Decrease Rnd 5: *K4, k2tog*; rep * to * around.
Knit 1 rnd.
Decrease Rnd 6: *K3, k2tog*; rep * to * around.
Knit 1 rnd.
Decrease Rnd 7: *K2, k2tog*; rep * to * around.
Knit 1 rnd.
Decrease Rnd 8: *K1, k2tog*; rep * to * around.
Knit 1 rnd.
Decrease Rnd 9: K2tog around.
Knit 1 rnd.
Decrease Rnd 10: K2tog around, ending with k1 = 7 sts rem.
- Cut yarn and draw end through rem sts; tighten.
- Beginning at center front, crochet edging all around "collar."
- Weave in all ends neatly on WS.
- Block by patting out cuddle bag to finished measurements and gently steam pressing on WS under a damp pressing cloth.

	= knit
x	= purl
o	= yo
/	= k2tog

X	X	X	X	X	X	X	X	X	X	X	X	X	X	X	X	X	X
/	/	/	o		o		o		o		o		o	/	/	/

Jackie

SIZE
0-3 months

MATERIALS
Yarn:
CYCA #1 (fingering) Viking Garn
Baby Ull (100% Merino wool, 191
yd/175 m / 50 g)
Yarn Colors and Amounts:
White 300: 200 g
Needles:
U. S. size 4 / 3.5 mm: 24 in / 60
cm circular and set of 5 dpn; cable
needle
Crochet Hook:
U. S. size B-1/C-2 / 2.5 mm for
edging

STITCHES AND TECHNIQUES
Seed Stitch
Row 1: *K1, p1*; rep * to * across.
Row 2: Work knit over purl and
purl over knit.
Rep Rows 1-2.

Pattern
See chart.

Crocheted Edging
1 sc, *ch 2, 1 dc in same st as sc, skip
⅜ in / 1 cm, 1 sc in next st*; rep
from * to * all around outer edge
of collar.

- CO 144 sts.
- Work back and forth in seed st for 6¾ in / 17 cm.
- Pm when 24 sts rem on needle. This will now be the beginning of rnd.
- Continue, working in the round.
- Work 48 sts of pattern following chart, centered across front of cuddle bag. Knit rem sts of rnd.
- Continue in pattern as est until cuddle bag is approx. 19¼ in / 49 cm long, including "collar." End with a complete pattern repeat.
- Pm at each side of cuddle bag with 72 sts for the front and 72 sts for back. You will now decrease on each side while the pattern is continued on the front as est.
- Decrease as follows: Work until 3 sts before marker, k2tog, kl, sl m, k1, ssk. Decrease the same way at each side on every other rnd until 48 sts rem on each side of markers = 96 sts total rem. End with a compete pattern repeat.
- Knit 1 rnd, stopping at last marker of rnd.
- Join bottom with 3-needle bind-off:
- Divide sts onto 2 needles, with 48 sts of front on one needle and 48 sts of back on second needle. Turn cuddle bag inside out. Hold needles parallel with RS facing RS. With a third needle, k2tog, joining first st on each needle. *K2tog joining first sts on left needle = 2 sts now on right needle. Pass 1st worked st over 2nd.* Rep from * to * until 1 st rem. Cut yarn and draw end through last st.
- Beginning at center front, crochet edging all around "collar."
- Weave in all ends neatly on WS.
- Block by laying blanket between two damp towels until completely dry.

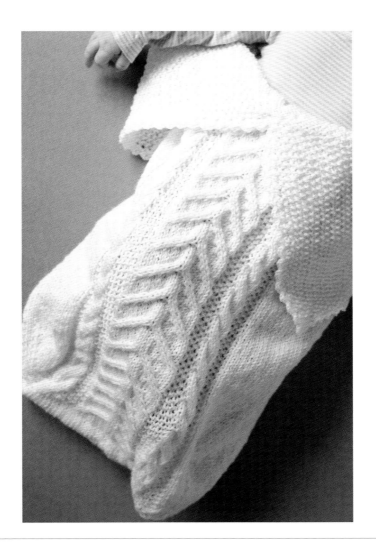

	= knit
x	= purl
---------->	= place 2 sts on cable needle and hold behind work, k2, k2 from cable needle.
<----------	= place 2 sts on cable needle and hold in front of work, k2, k2 from cable needle.
------------------>	= place 3 sts on cable needle and hold behind work, k3, k3 from cable needle.
<------------------	= place 3 sts on cable needle and hold in front of work, k3, k3 from cable needle.

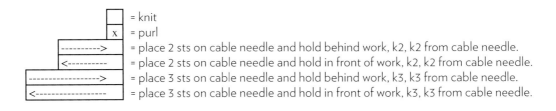

Acknowledgments

Thank you to Elen Zickfeldt.
Thank you to Studio Hjelm in Stavanger for the lovely photos.
Thank you to Movio Fredrik Helliesen for converting the charts.
Thank you to my family and friends for your inspiration and support.
A special thanks to Bjørn, Ida, Håkon, Anne-Mari, Torunn, Åse Marie, and Jannicke

Yarn Information

Some Dale Garn yarns may be available from:
Yarn Cupboard
yarncupboard.com

Garnstudio yarns may be purchased from retailers listed by:
Garnstudio
garnstudio.com

Sandnes yarns may be purchased (with international shipping charges) from:
Scandinavian Knitting Design
scandinavianknittingdesign.com

Some yarns and materials—Gjestal and Viking yarns, in particular—may be difficult to find. A variety of additional and substitute yarns are available from:
Webs – America's Yarn Store
75 Service Center Road
Northampton, MA 01060
800-367-9327
yarn.com

LoveKnitting.com
loveknitting.com/us

If you are unable to obtain any of the yarn used in this book, it can be replaced with a yarn of a similar weight and composition. Please note, however, the finished projects may vary slightly from those shown, depending on the yarn used. Try www.yarnsub.com for suggestions.

For more information on selecting or substituting yarn, contact your local yarn shop or an online store; they are familiar with all types of yarns and would be happy to help you. Additionally, the online knitting community at Ravelry.com has forums where you can post questions about specific yarns. Yarns come and go so quickly these days and there are so many beautiful yarns available.